Complete EnglishSmart

Grade **3**

Desmond Gilling • Marilyn Kennedy • Joanne Igercich

ISBN : 1-894810-66-X

Copyright © 2006 **Popular Book Company (Canada) Limited**

Printed in China

Complete EnglishSmart Contents

Integrated Practice

Nunavut, Canada's Newest Territory

Originally, Canada was made up of ten provinces and two northern territories called the Yukon and the Northwest Territories. On April 1, 1999, the Northwest Territories was divided into two parts. The new area to the east was called Nunavut.

Nunavut has the largest land area in Canada. It is almost 2,000,000 sq. km in area and makes up 1/5 of Canada. The capital of Nunavut is Iqaluit with a population of 4,000. Some villages in Nunavut have as few as 18 residents.

Because much of Nunavut is above the Arctic Circle, winter lasts about 9 months and is extremely cold. Most of Nunavut's soil is called "permafrost", which means that it stays frozen all year round. In spring and summer, the sun does not set and there is daylight 24 hours a day.

Most of the people that live in Nunavut are Inuit. In the Inuktitut language, Inuit means "people". There are about 25,000 people living in Nunavut today. People use snowmobiles and planes to travel around in Nunavut. In the old days, the Inuit used dogsleds as the main form of transportation. They hunted for food and made their clothing from the hides of animals.

The seal was the most important animal to the Inuit. They made boots from sealskin and used the blubber for both lamp oil and food. A favourite food was "muktuk" – the blubber from whales. Today, half the population still hunt and fish for their food.

Finding Information

A. Answer the following questions by finding information from the passage.

1. What are the names of Canada's original territories before Nunavut?

    _____

2. Name the capital of Nunavut.

    _____

3. What is the total population of Nunavut?

    _____

4. Why are Nunavut's winters so cold?

    _____

5. How long does winter last?

    _____

6. Why is Nunavut's soil called "permafrost"?

    _____

7. What are the two methods of transportation used in Nunavut?

    _____

8. What language do the Inuit people of Nunavut speak?

    _____

9. How did the Inuit people travel in the old days?

    _____

10. Which Arctic animal was the most important to the Inuit?

    _____

Nouns

- A Common Noun is a person, place, thing, or idea.

  Examples: person — boy, girl, man, woman

  place — house, school, store, building, farm

  thing — car, book, plant, bicycle, doll, computer

  idea — friendship, happiness, truth, feelings, thoughts

- A Proper Noun is the actual name of a person, place, or thing.

  Examples: person — John A. Macdonald, Wayne Gretzky, Britney Spears

  place — Toronto, Sky Dome, Royal Ontario Museum, St. Joseph's School, Lake Ontario, Rocky Mountains

  thing — Chrysler, Barbie Doll, Kleenex

B. Put the nouns into the correct columns.

baby	room	Moon River	task	park
citizen	Mrs. Jones	effort	desk	pen
player	lake	leaf	lie	Dr. Smith
owner	road	sweater	Backstreet Boys	promise
school	manager	CN Tower	stick	truck
farm	child	help	Mt. Albert	joy

Person	Place	Thing	Idea	Proper Noun

Consonants

- *A Consonant is any letter that is not a vowel (a,e,i,o,u).*

C. Solve the consonant riddles. Place the consonant letters in the spaces provided.

1. I'm a consonant that has a buzz. .... ☐

2. I can do this with my eyes wide open. .... ☐

3. I drink this in the morning instead of coffee. .... ☐

4. I like this kind of soup. .... ☐

5. I line up in one of these. .... ☐

6. I am the plural of the verb "is". .... ☐

7. Sometimes I mark the spot. .... ☐

8. I'm a blue bird and a baseball player. .... ☐

Missing Consonants

D. Add consonants to the vowels below. Try to form three words for each vowel.

1.	2.	3.
_____ u _____	_____ i _____	_____ o _____
_____ u _____	_____ i _____	_____ o _____
_____ u _____	_____ i _____	_____ o _____

4.	5.	6.
_____ oo _____	_____ e _____	_____ ea _____
_____ oo _____	_____ e _____	_____ ea _____
_____ oo _____	_____ e _____	_____ ea _____

What Makes up Our Universe?

Astronomers are scientists that study the universe. Some astronomers believe that at one time, all the stars and planets were joined together in one big lump. They think that the universe began as a result of a big explosion that happened about 15 billion years ago. They call this event the Big Bang.

It is thought that this explosion sent pieces of the universe flying off in various directions. As time passed, some of these pieces drifted together and formed galaxies. These galaxies continue to travel in space, making the universe bigger and bigger as time passes.

Astronomers have different ideas about the future of the universe. Some believe that it will continue to grow. Others think that the galaxies will drift back towards each other, reversing the Big Bang.

We live in a galaxy called the Milky Way. When you look at the sky on a clear night, you can see the stars and planets that make up the Milky Way. The Milky Way got its name because it looks like a white stream of light. There are about 1,000 billion stars in the Milky Way but most of them we cannot see.

It is believed that there are 100 billion galaxies in the universe. It is impossible to know how many billions of stars make up the entire universe. But, astronomers think that there are about 100 million trillion!

Matching Facts

A. Match the information in Column A with the explanations in Column B.

Column A

1. Milky Way ⬭
2. galaxy ⬭
3. astronomers ⬭
4. 1,000 billion ⬭
5. Big Bang ⬭
6. 100 billion ⬭

Column B

A it happened 15 billion years ago

B the galaxy that we live in

C number of stars in a galaxy

D scientists that study the universe

E number of galaxies in the universe

F a collection of stars and planets

Further Thought

B. Answer the following questions.

1. Can you explain in your own words the Big Bang theory?

   _____

   _____

   _____

   _____

2. How did the Milky Way get its name?

   _____

   _____

   _____

   _____

Verbs

- A Verb is an action word in a sentence. It shows what the subject of the sentence is doing.

  Example: The boy ran home. "Ran" is the verb in this sentence.

C. Underline the verb in each sentence below.

At The Hockey Game

1. The hockey player shot the puck at the net.

2. The goalie fell to the ice.

3. The goalie missed the puck.

4. The crowd cheered wildly.

5. The player raised his arms in celebration.

D. Place a verb that would make sense for each sentence below. Try not to use the same verb twice.

dribbled	helped	called	swung	played
exercised	bounced	chased	gathered	asked

1. The pupils _____ in the school yard.

2. They _____ on the monkey bars.

3. Some boys _____ basketball.

4. Some of the girls _____ the younger students.

5. A few children _____ balls.

6. The teacher _____ everyone to return to class.

Vowels

- The Vowels – a, e, i, o, u – can have long or short vowel sounds.

  Examples: cat – has a short "a" vowel sound
             plate – has a long vowel sound

  Note: the long vowel sound sounds out the actual letter.

E. Underline the vowel in each word and write "short" or "long" in the space following the word.

1. plate _____

2. duck _____

3. come _____

4. may _____

5. stone _____

6. toe _____

7. pop _____

8. clue _____

9. throw _____

F. Eavesdropping ... Can you figure out what the children are saying? Just fill in the vowels.

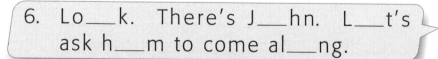

1. It is a b___a___tif___l d___y today.

2. Y___s, it ___s. Sh___ll we go o___ts___de?

3. L___t's go to th___ p___rk.

4. Wo___ld you l___ke to c___me t_____?

5. Th___nk yo___ f___r ask___ng m___ to jo___n you.

6. Lo___k. There's J___hn. L___t's ask h___m to come al___ng.

7. I'd l___ve to g___ to th___ p___rk. Sh___ll I br___ng a s___cc___r b___ll?

Are We Alone in the Universe?

Scientists and astronomers have argued over whether or not there is life on other planets. It could be possible because there are other galaxies that could have a sun like ours. These planets could have water and enough warmth to allow for life to exist.

One answer to this question may lie in the large number of UFO sightings. UFO stands for "Unidentified Flying Object". There are over 100 reported UFO sightings daily. Many of these can be explained as weather balloons, research aircraft, or reflections from the sun. Some scientists believe that many of these sightings are real UFOs. They believe that extra-terrestrials (beings from other planets) are trying to visit us or make contact with us. Imagine meeting beings from another planet. Think of what knowledge we could share and how much we could learn.

There are people who believe that they have been captured by aliens. They reported that aliens came to them while they were sleeping and took them into a spaceship. None of them reported being harmed. However, none of these cases have been proven.

Perhaps we are not alone. Perhaps those people who claim to have seen UFOs actually did see them. If so, there will be interesting encounters in space in the future.

Remembering Details

A. Fill in the blanks with suitable words.

There could be life on another planet if it has a 1._____ like ours. For life to exist, a planet needs 2._____ and 3._____. Every day, there are over 4._____ reports from people who think that they have seen an Unidentified Flying Object. A being from another planet is called an 5._____. These beings would probably travel in 6._____. Some people believe that they have been 7._____ by aliens but they were not 8._____.

An Interview with an Alien

B. Pretend that you are interviewing an alien. Write the questions that you want to ask your alien visitor.

You might use "Who / What / Where / When / Why" to make questions.

Question 1. _____

_____

Question 2. _____

_____

Question 3. _____

_____

Question 4. _____

A Picture of My Alien

_____

Possessive Nouns

- A Possessive Noun shows ownership.

  Example: *If John owns a bicycle, you might state: This is John's bicycle.*

- *Notice that to show ownership, you add an apostrophe (') and the letter "s".*

- *Here are three important rules of possessive nouns:*
  1. *If the noun is singular, add 's — The boy's baseball ...*
  2. *If the noun ends in the letter "s", add 's — The actress's part in the play ...*
  3. *If the noun is plural, that is, it has an "s" already added to make it plural, add only the apostrophe (') — The horses' hooves could be heard in the distance ...*

C. Make the changes needed to make the nouns possessive. Place 's or ' in the spaces provided beside the nouns.

| Example | Here is Paul___ coat. ⟶ Here is Paul_'s_ coat. |

1. These are the aliens___ spaceships.

2. The little alien___ neck is very long.

3. At school, there is a boys___ washroom on the first floor.

4. There is a girls___ washroom on the second floor.

5. Jim___ dog followed him to school.

6. They played in the children___ yard.

7. The coaches___ whistles blew at the same time.

8. James___ team won the game.

9. The coach was happy with the children___ performance.

10. One girl___ scream could be heard above all the rest.

11. The girls___ cheers were heard throughout the gymnasium.

12. Julie___ friend came with her to the game.

The Silent "e" and the Long Vowel

- *When we add a silent "e" to a word, the vowel in the word changes from short to long.*

  Example: The name Tim, which has the short vowel sound ĭ changes to the long vowel sound ī.

  Notice that this little change also changes the whole meaning of the word. Instead of the name Tim, we now have the word "time".

D. Drop the silent "e" in each underlined word. Match the new words with the appropriate meanings.

The Camping Trip

Last summer, our family went camping. We found a spot under a <u>huge</u> <u>pine</u> tree and pitched our tent. After the work, we had a <u>bite</u> to eat. We <u>ate</u> sandwiches and <u>ripe</u> apples. We decided to <u>use</u> the branches of the trees to hang up our towels. We saw a <u>cute</u> chipmunk and watched it <u>hide</u> behind a leaf. We used <u>tape</u> to hang up our garbage bag. We ate an ice <u>cube</u> to cool off. At night we <u>made</u> a <u>fire</u>.

1. couldn't be seen – _____

2. wrap your arms around – _____

3. slice in two – _____

4. you and me – _____

5. just a little, a – _____

6. to tear – _____

7. touch lightly – _____

8. needle and – _____

9. shows where – _____

10. angry – _____

11. a baby bear – _____

12. a type of tree – _____

The Simpsons (1)

"**D**on't have a cow, man!" Do you recognize these words? Yes, these are the words of Bart Simpson, the most popular cartoon character on television. But do you know how *The Simpsons* was created?

The creator of *The Simpsons* is Matt Groening. He grew up in Portland, Oregon, on the <u>west</u> <u>coast</u> of the United States. Matt was one of five children. All the Simpson characters, except Bart, were named after members of Groening's family. The name Bart is an anagram (a word with letters rearranged from another word). If you rearrange the letters in the word "brat", you get Bart, which is a fitting description of the mischievous cartoon character.

When Matt Groening was a little <u>boy</u>, he wanted to do something for a living that was fun. Often, he would get into trouble at <u>school</u> for drawing sketches when he was supposed to be doing schoolwork. As a college student, he drew cartoons for the college newspaper.

Once he graduated, Groening went to California to look for work. He got a job as a cartoonist on a small paper. The lady who sold advertising for that newspaper told him that his <u>cartoons</u> were the most <u>popular</u> part of the newspaper. That lady, named Deborah, later became his <u>wife</u>. They left the newspaper and worked on a comic strip entitled *Life in Hell*. Matt <u>drew</u> the comic strip while Deborah sold the cartoons to different newspapers and <u>magazines</u>. They were making some money, but the real <u>wealth</u> lay ahead.

Recalling Facts

A. **Place "T" for true and "F" for false beside each of the following statements in the space provided.**

1. Bart is the name of one of Groening's brothers. .... ☐

2. Groening was brought up in California. .... ☐

3. Groening used his own family as a model for *The Simpsons*. .... ☐

4. Groening was a cartoon artist in college. .... ☐

5. Groening met his wife in college. .... ☐

6. Groening's wife, Deborah, worked at the same newspaper
   as he did. .... ☐

7. When the Groenings quit working at the newspaper, they
   made a living with comic strips. .... ☐

8. The Groenings made a fortune drawing cartoons for the
   Life in Hell comic strip. .... ☐

Your Opinion

B. **Give short answers to the following questions.**

1. How does the fact that Matt Groening grew up in a large family help
   him in creating *The Simpsons* television series?

   _____

   _____

2. What two qualities do you think Matt Groening has that make him a
   good cartoonist?

   _____

   _____

Pronouns

- Pronouns are words that are used to take the place of nouns.

  Examples: 1. This is <u>John's</u> hat.   The hat is <u>his</u>.
  2. <u>Jennifer</u> was late for school.   <u>She</u> was late for school.
  3. <u>Denise and Paula</u> sang a song.   <u>They</u> sang a song.
  4. <u>Brian and I</u> went to the store.   <u>We</u> went to the store.

  In the examples above, the underlined words are related because the first is a noun, and the second is the pronoun replacing the noun.

C. Underline the pronouns in the following sentences.

> The number at the end of each sentence tells you how many pronouns to underline.

1. Jeff and I played hockey together.   (1)

2. He helped him with the homework.   (2)

3. The car would not start, so we had it repaired.   (2)

4. We saw them running to catch the bus.   (2)

5. The teacher gave me help with my spelling.   (2)

D. In each sentence below, choose the best pronoun to suit the sentence.

1. We / Us _____ are going to walk home together.

2. Me / I _____ like eating popcorn at the movies.

3. Him / He _____ is in my class.

4. She / Her _____ is my best friend.

5. Paul tossed she / me _____ the basketball.

Word Study Crosswords

E. Use the underlined words in the passage to solve the puzzles.

Crossword A

Across

A. not east
B. like books, but have lots of pictures

Down

1. riches, or not as good as health
2. opposite of husband
3. made a picture

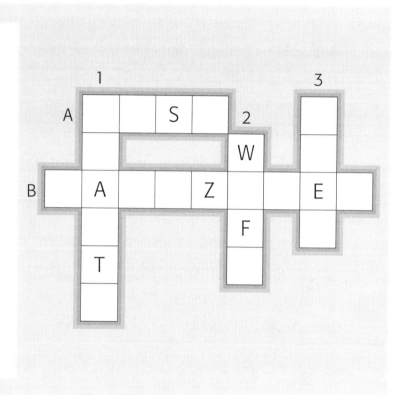

Crossword B

Across

1. comics on TV
2. a place to learn

Down

A. not a girl
B. well-liked, well-known
C. by the water's edge

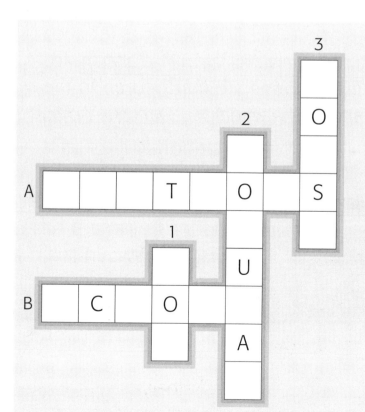

The Simpsons (2)

James Brooks, a television producer, was a fan of the *Life in Hell* comic strip. He was looking for a 20-second "filler" on one of his television shows. He asked Groening to create something like the comic characters in *Life in Hell*. Groening came up with *The Simpsons*.

When *The Simpsons* first appeared on television in 1989, it became very popular. Brooks asked the owners of the television network if they could create a half-hour comedy cartoon. The network bosses liked the idea, and *The Simpsons* was given a chance. Groening and Brooks knew it was a risk because it had been over 20 years since a cartoon show was a success. The first Simpsons show was called "The Simpsons Roasting on an Open Fire". It went on television on December 17, 1989 as a Christmas show. It was a huge success.

Each half-hour show takes about six months to create. There is a team of 50 cartoonists that make 2,000 drawings for each show. Groening spends his time supervising them. He also makes sure that the people speaking the parts are matched up to the mouth movements of the cartoon characters.

Deborah and Matt Groening have become very wealthy since *The Simpsons* became a hit television show. In fact, they named their first child Homer, in honour of the famous Simpson father.

Recognizing Details

A. Circle the correct answer in each of the following statements.

1. The television producer that put *The Simpsons* on television was
    A. Matt Groening.   B. James Brooks.   C. Deborah Groening.

2. At first, *The Simpsons* was on for only
    A. 20 seconds.   B. 40 minutes.   C. 30 minutes.

3. The first Simpsons show went on television on
    A. January 1, 1995.   B. April 1, 1990.   C. December 17, 1989.

4. To create each show, it takes
    A. 6 months.   B. 1 year.   C. 3 weeks.

5. The number of drawings for each show is
    A. 5,000.   B. 500.   C. 2,000.

6. The number of artists working on the drawings for *The Simpsons* is
    A. 25.   B. 50.   C. 100.

7. The Groenings named their first child
    A. Homer.   B. Bart.   C. Ned.

8. The first Simpsons show was
    A. a Halloween show. B. an Easter show.   C. a Christmas show.

9. *The Simpsons* was the first successful cartoon show on television
    A. in over 20 years.   B. in over 2 years.   C. in over 50 years.

10. Because of the success of *The Simpsons*, the Groenings became
    A. very proud.   B. very wealthy.   C. very tired.

Pronouns

- *Like the nouns they replace, Pronouns can also show ownership.*

  Example: This is Jack's cap. This is his cap.

B. **Rewrite the following sentences. Replace the underlined words with pronouns.**

its	his	her	mine	yours	theirs	hers

1. Here is <u>Bob's</u> cat.   Here is his cat.

2. Joanne dropped <u>Lisa's</u> book.   _____

3. Fido is <u>the dog's</u> name.   _____

4. The hat is <u>Mrs. Jones's</u>.   _____

5. That book is <u>your book</u>.   _____

6. This house is <u>my house</u>.   _____

7. The toys are <u>Sam's and Justin's</u>.   _____

8. The new shoes are <u>John's</u>.   _____

> *Some vowels have the same sound even though they are different letters.*

Rhyming Words

C. **Make new words with similar vowel sounds that rhyme. Use the clues to help you.**

1. eaten	2. drift
_____ lose the game _____ add sugar	_____ a present _____ to pick up

3. otter	4. ore
_____ more heat	_____ noise when sleeping
_____ goes with "fly"	_____ a job around the house
_____ Harry's last name	_____ place to buy candy
5. giver	6. cow
_____ body part	_____ above your eyes
_____ flows	_____ word for food
_____ wood in your finger	_____ at this time
_____ shake when cold	_____ work in the field
7. chew	8. kept
_____ make coffee	_____ went slowly
_____ took to the air	_____ cried
_____ sticky stuff	_____ cleaned the floor
_____ one for each foot	_____ went to bed

You may make all the lines rhyme or use rhyming pairs of lines.

Write a Verse of Poetry

D. Use your rhyming words to create a four-line verse of poetry.

_____

_____

_____

_____

6 Water Safety

There is nothing quite as refreshing as a cool dip in the water on a hot, <u>humid</u> summer day. It is fun to swim in a pool, a river, or a lake. However, playing in water can be <u>dangerous</u> if you don't know the rules of water safety.

The first <u>rule</u> of water safety is to always swim with a <u>buddy</u>. If you have a <u>problem</u>, the friend can help you or run to get help. Besides, it is always more fun if you have a friend to play with in the water. It is best to have an adult present, especially if you are not a good swimmer. Never swim at a beach where there is no lifeguard or adult present.

Swimming pools are usually well <u>supervised</u> but you can still get injured. Most injuries are a result of children running and slipping on wet pool <u>surfaces</u>. If you are a beginning swimmer, always stay in the shallow end of the pool.

If you swim in a river or lake, be sure to <u>investigate</u> what is below the water surface. Often there are rocks or branches hidden in the water. If you jump or dive into unknown waters, you may seriously injure yourself on a hidden object.

If you are at a cottage, you may have the chance to go boating as well as swimming. It is important to always wear a lifejacket when in a boat.

Swimming and boating are among the most <u>enjoyable</u> summer activities. Protect yourself by following these basic rules of safety.

Summarizing Information

A. In the passage, there are six rules of safety. Write each rule in your own words.

Write as many rules of safety as you can remember before looking back at the passage.

Rule #1: _____

Rule #2: _____

Rule #3: _____

Rule #4: _____

Rule #5: _____

Rule #6: _____

B. Pretend you are a lifeguard at the local swimming pool. Make a sign with important safety rules for your pool. Give your sign a catchy title.

Adjectives

- *Adjectives are words that describe nouns. They tell something about a noun and help us know more about the noun they are describing.*

  Example: The <u>playful</u> kitten jumped up.

  "Playful" is an adjective that describes the kitten.

C. Underline the adjectives in the following sentences.

The number following each sentence tells how many adjectives are in the sentence.

1. The dark night frightened the young children. (2)

2. Wear a warm hat and a winter coat. (2)

3. Wild animals belong in their natural habitat. (2)

4. Old Mr. Smith still plays a good round of golf. (2)

5. Be careful when crossing a busy street, especially on a slippery road. (3)

 Using Adjectives

D. Fill in the blanks by choosing adjectives that fit the meanings of the sentences.

| excited | birthday | icy | furry | cold | happy | white |

1. The _____ dog sheds hair on the furniture.

2. The _____ steps were slippery.

3. A _____ wind blew as the _____ snow fell.

4. The _____ child opened her _____ gifts.

5. We all sang _____ Birthday To You.

Understanding Words in Sentences

- One way to figure out the meaning of a word is to read the sentence in which the word appears. The information in the sentence will help you understand the meaning of the word.

E. Look back to the passage and find the underlined words listed below. Match the words in Column A with the meanings in Column B.

Column A	Column B
1. humid	A good friend
2. dangerous	B difficulty
3. rule	C being watched
4. buddy	D the tops of things
5. problem	E hot and sticky weather
6. supervised	F lots of fun
7. surfaces	G not very safe
8. investigate	H thing to obey
9. enjoyable	I look into; find out about

F. Answer the questions.

1. Three words above have four vowels. Can you list these words?

   A. _____   B. _____   C. _____

2. Which word has five vowels?   _____

Accidental Inventions

Not all inventions were meant to happen. In some cases, people made mistakes that ended up becoming inventions. They accidentally invented something useful or interesting.

The Popsicle was the result of a mistake. In 1905, an eleven-year-old boy named Frank Epperson was trying to make a flavourful drink. He mixed soda pop powder with water and left it on his back porch overnight. It froze with the stir stick stuck in the middle. The next day he pulled it out and tasted the frozen drink. It was an instant hit. He called it the "Epperson Icicle" and sold them in his neighbourhood for five cents each. He later named the invention "popsicle".

A year before the invention of the popsicle, the ice cream cone was invented. One very hot afternoon at the 1904 St. Louis World's Fair, a young man was selling a lot of ice cream. Soon he ran out of paper ice cream cups and had nothing to put his ice cream in. He was desperate to find something in which to serve his ice cream. Then he noticed an Arab vendor selling wafer-like biscuits sprinkled with sugar. He bought a stack of these wafers and started putting ice cream inside them. He sold his ice cream on the cone-like wafers. This new way to serve ice cream soon became very popular.

Both these cases prove that the old expression, *Necessity is the Mother of Invention*, is certainly true.

Understanding Story Ideas

Sometimes there is a reason we invent things.

A. **Write what you think the expression,**
Necessity is the Mother of Invention, means.

_____

_____

Using Facts - Making Inferences

B. **Answer the questions.**

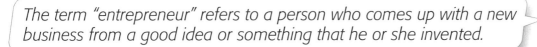
The term "entrepreneur" refers to a person who comes up with a new business from a good idea or something that he or she invented.

1. Why can we say that Frank Epperson was an "entrepreneur"?

   _____

   _____

2. How was the invention of the ice cream cone an accident?

   _____

   _____

3. Are you an inventor? Do you have a great idea for something new? Describe your invention and draw a picture of it.

✏ Name of invention _____	
✏ What it is made of _____	
✏ What it does _____	
_____	
✏ Who would use it _____	
✏ How much it would cost _____	

Adverbs

- *An Adverb describes the verb (action word) in a sentence. It tells something about the verb, such as how an action takes place. Adverbs often end in "ly".*

C. **Fill in adverbs that best describe the action words (verbs) in the paragraph below. Choose your adverbs from the choices in parentheses.**

The Basketball Game

In a basketball game, there is a lot of action.

The players leaped (high, low) 1._____ at centre court

for the jump ball to start the game. The player on the Raptors (skilfully,

carelessly) 2._____ dribbled the ball past the defender.

He jumped in the air and shot the ball (directly, nearly)

3._____ at the basket. The ball did not go in and the

Grizzlies (noisily, quickly) 4._____ grabbed the rebound.

The player on the Raptors (slowly, cleverly) 5._____ stole

the ball from the opposition and ran (swiftly,

smartly) 6._____ down the court.

The referee blew his whistle (loudly, silently)

7._____ and the play (immediately,

never) 8._____ stopped. The

fans booed the referee (loudly, quietly)

9._____ when he called a foul on

the Raptor player.

Digraphs

- Digraphs are two letters that, when placed together, make a single sound.

  Examples: 1. rain – the "ai" gives the sound of a long ā.
  play – the "ay" gives the sound of a long ā.

  2. feed – the "ee" gives the sound of a long ē.
  each – the "ea" gives the sound of a long ē.

  3. boat – the "oa" gives the sound of a long ō.

D. Unscramble the mixed-up letters to make proper words.

All of these have digraphs. Put those letters together first and the rest is easy. A clue to the meaning of each proper word is provided for you.

#	Scrambled	Answer	Clue
1.	e r a h c	r e a c h	stretch your arm out
2.	t e m e		get together with a friend
3.	a t m e		put it on the barbecue
4.	m e t a		all the players together
5.	o t a c		goes with the hat
6.	y t a s		don't go
7.	i s l a		you need a boat
8.	i t b a		you can get hooked on this
9.	t y a r s		sometimes cats or dogs
10.	o t s a t		a quick breakfast
11.	r e f i d n		your buddy

The Second Most Popular Drink in the World

The most popular drink in the world is, of course, water. But what is the second most popular drink? If you guessed milk, you would be wrong. It is tea.

Tea was invented about 4,700 years ago. A Chinese emperor, Shen Nung, was boiling water under a tree when a few leaves fell into his drink. He noticed a pleasant smell coming from the cup. He tasted it, and from that moment on, tea became a drink.

Tea became popular in Europe in 1610. Up until about 200 years ago, tea was actually used for money in some Asian countries. People would buy things with a block of tea or carve off a piece of the block for smaller, less expensive purchases.

The most popular form of tea is the tea bag. It was invented by Thomas Sullivan, a tea and coffee merchant. One day, he decided to send samples of tea wrapped in little silk bags to his customers. Much to his surprise, when the orders arrived for his tea, his customers insisted that the tea be wrapped in these little silk bags. The idea of the tea bag was born. Today, more than half the tea in the world is bought this way.

Each year, there are over 800 billion cups of tea consumed worldwide. Perhaps, if Thomas Sullivan hadn't accidentally invented the tea bag, tea would not have been so popular.

Choosing Correct Facts

A. **In each group, place a check mark beside the correct fact. First, answer the questions without looking back at the story. Then, reread the story to check your answers.**

1. A. The most popular drink in the world is water. ☐

   B. The most popular drink in the world is tea. ☐

   C. The most popular drink in the world is milk. ☐

2. A. An Emperor of China discovered tea. ☐

   B. The Queen of England discovered tea. ☐

   C. An ancient king discovered tea. ☐

3. A. Tea was also used for growing plants. ☐

   B. Tea was also used as money. ☐

   C. Tea was also used as decoration. ☐

4. A. Thomas Sullivan who invented tea bags was a merchant. ☐

   B. Thomas Sullivan who invented tea bags was a sailor. ☐

   C. Thomas Sullivan who invented tea bags was an explorer. ☐

5. A. The first tea bag was made of cloth. ☐

   B. The first tea bag was made of paper. ☐

   C. The first tea bag was made of silk. ☐

6. A. Tea was invented 4,700 years ago. ☐

   B. Tea was invented 800 billion years ago. ☐

   C. Tea was invented 2,700 years ago. ☐

The Simple Sentence

- A simple sentence is made up of a Subject and a Predicate.
- The Subject contains a noun and sometimes an adjective (a word that describes the noun).
- The Predicate contains a verb (the action performed by the noun subject) and sometimes an adverb (a word that describes a verb).

Examples:
1. The dog barked loudly.
   "The dog" is the subject and "barked loudly" is the predicate.
2. The happy child laughed out loud.
   The subject is "the happy child". The predicate is "laughed out loud".

B. For each sentence below, draw a line between the subject and the predicate.

1. The girls played volleyball.
2. His parents went out.
3. They watched television together.
4. The fast runner won the race.
5. The first person in the gym turned on the lights.

C. Complete the sentences with your own predicates.

1. The hockey players _____ .
2. The kitten _____ .
3. My father and I _____ .
4. The students in grade three _____ .
5. The helpful girls _____ .

D. Complete the sentences with your own subjects.

1. _____ played in the park.
2. _____ were late for school.

3. _____ bought a new car.

4. _____ was the high scorer in the game.

5. _____ watched a scary movie together.

Consonant Blends

- A Consonant Blend is formed when two consonants placed together form a blended sound.

E. Read the hints. Fill in the blanks with suitable consonant blends.

bl	cl	ch	br	sh	cr	py	tr

1.	__ __ e e d	2.	__ __ u e s
	after a cut		help solve puzzles
3.	__ __ i c k	4.	s l e e __ __
	baby chicken		feeling tired
5.	__ __ i c k	6.	__ __ a b
	or treat		crawls underwater
7.	__ __ i c k	8.	w a __ __
	for building		do with water

F. Build rhyming words from consonant blends.

beach   walk   fast   lick   skim   stay

1. _____ 2. _____ 3. _____ 4. _____ 5. _____ 6. _____

snore   spill   trip   snap   friend   crack

7. _____ 8. _____ 9. _____ 10. _____ 11. _____ 12. _____

Fossils – The Link to the Dinosaur

Dinosaurs roamed the earth over 200 million years ago. About 70 million years ago, they completely disappeared. We learn about dinosaurs from fossils. Fossils are found in rocks.

Rocks tell the story of the earth's history. If we look at the edge of a cliff, we will notice that there are many layers of rock. These layers may be of different colour and thickness. The layers closest to the earth's surface are the oldest. As time passed, new layers of rock settled on older layers.

In between these layers of rock, the skeleton remains of animals were pressed. As years passed and more rock layers piled up, these remains became impressions in the rock. It is these impressions that tell us about the dinosaurs.

The type of rock layer will reveal the time period in the earth's history. The fossil will show the kind of animal that lived at that time because the skeleton remains were imbedded there. From both these facts, we can trace the time period that a certain animal lived. Leaf fossils found in rocks tell us what plants covered the earth at certain time periods. Therefore, we can also figure out the plant life that the dinosaurs would have depended on for food.

To understand fossils, think of a fresh piece of sidewalk concrete. If you walked on it, you would create the shape of your feet and the length of your step. If thousands of years from now, someone found your footprints in this concrete slab, what would they be able to figure out about you? They would know your shoe size, your height, your weight, and how you walked. This is the same way fossils tell the tale of dinosaurs.

The Main Idea of a Paragraph

• *The Main Idea of a paragraph is the most important fact or idea that the paragraph tells us.*

A. Place a check mark in the space beside the statement that tells the main idea of each paragraph from the passage.

Paragraph One

A. Dinosaurs roamed the earth. .... ☐

B. We learn about dinosaurs from fossils. .... ☐

C. Dinosaurs are extinct. .... ☐

Paragraph Two

A. Rocks tell the earth's history. .... ☐

B. The earth is very rocky. .... ☐

C. There are many layers of rock in a cliff. .... ☐

Paragraph Three

A. Animals were crushed in rocks. .... ☐

B. Many rock layers piled up. .... ☐

C. Skeletal impressions tell about dinosaur history. .... ☐

Paragraph Four

A. Fossils tell us about both plant and animal life. .... ☐

B. Leaves can be fossils too. .... ☐

C. Dinosaurs ate plants. .... ☐

Paragraph Five

A. Concrete is like a layer of rock. .... ☐

B. Footprints in concrete are like fossils. .... ☐

C. Wet concrete leaves marks. .... ☐

Creating Simple Sentences

B. **Unscramble each group of words to make a proper sentence. Remember to look for a subject and a predicate.**

1. the   world   years   dinosaurs   roamed   many   ago

   _____

2. holidays   summer   finally   here   are

   _____

3. game   the   we   won

   _____

4. the   test   gave   teacher   pupils   a   the

   _____

5. cream   ice   he   two   ate   scoops   of

   _____

6. long   it   day   rained   all

   _____

C. **Match the subjects with the suitable predicates.**

Subject	Predicate
1. The old man	A gathered in the school gymnasium
2. The crying baby	B walked with a cane
3. The policeman	C made a lot of noise
4. All the students in grade three	D chased the thief

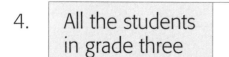

Consonant Blends with Three Letters

. . . .

- *Some Consonant Blends are made up of three consonant letters placed together.*

D. Write the three-letter consonants to form the words below. Use the clues to help you find the correct letters.

1.	_ _ _ e a d	put butter on your bread
2.	_ _ _ e a m	a small river
3.	_ _ _ e a m	a frightful sound
4.	_ _ _ e w	tossed the ball
5.	_ _ _ a w	use it with a drink
6.	_ _ _ a r e	not a circle
7.	_ _ _ e e t	where you live
8.	_ _ _ i n g	found in a mattress

Triple Consonant Crossword

E. Solve the crossword puzzle.

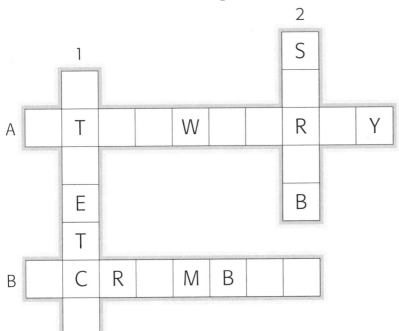

Down

1. pull apart
2. wipe clean

Across

A. a red fruit
B. a way to cook eggs

True or False

A. Mark "T" for true and "F" for false in the space provided beside each statement about the information in the passages.

There are 11 true answers and 14 false ones.

1. Originally Canada was made up of nine provinces and two territories. .... ☐

2. Permafrost means that the ground is always frozen. .... ☐

3. The seal was the most important animal to the Inuit. .... ☐

4. A scientist that studies the universe is called an astronomer. .... ☐

5. We live in a galaxy called the White Way. .... ☐

6. UFO stands for "Unidentified Foreign Object". .... ☐

7. Alien refers to a living being from another planet. .... ☐

8. Warmth and water are needed for a planet to have life. .... ☐

9. The creator of *The Simpsons* is James Brooks. .... ☐

10. The creator of *The Simpsons* was always in trouble at school. ...... ☐

11. Matt Groening is the television producer of *The Simpsons*. .... ☐

12. A half-hour show takes two weeks to make. .... ☐

13. The creator of *The Simpsons* named his first son Bart. .... ☐

14. It is okay to swim at a beach without a lifeguard. .... ☐

15. Pool surfaces are slippery when wet. .... ☐

16. If you are in a small boat, you do not need a lifejacket. .... ☐

17. Popsicles were invented in 1975. .... ☐

18. Frank Epperson accidentally invented a popsicle by freezing a
    drink with a stick in it. .... ☐

19. Ice cream cones were invented at the Olympics in 1904. .... ☐

20. The most popular drink in the world is milk. .... ☐

21. Tea was invented by a Chinese emperor. .... ☐

22. The tea bag is the most popular way that tea is sold today. .... ☐

23. Fossils are impressions in rock. .... ☐

24. The earth is made up of layers of rock. .... ☐

25. Only animals would leave fossils in rocks. .... ☐

B. **There are nouns, pronouns, verbs, adjectives, and adverbs in the following passage. Put the underlined words in the columns under the proper headings.**

<u>It</u> <u>was</u> a <u>bright</u>, <u>sunny</u> <u>morning</u> when the students <u>reported</u> to <u>school</u> for the <u>first</u> <u>time</u>. <u>They</u> were all <u>happy</u> to be in school <u>again</u>. They <u>anxiously</u> <u>waited</u> for the first <u>homework</u> assignment. When recess came, they <u>ran</u> <u>quickly</u> out to the huge <u>playground</u>. They <u>picked</u> two equal <u>teams</u> and <u>started</u> a <u>furious</u> game of touch football.

Noun	Pronoun	Verb	Adjective	Adverb

C. **Rewrite the words to make them possessive.**

1. This is   he   _____ desk.

2. He borrowed   Jane   _____ pencil.

3. The   waitress   _____ apron was dirty.

4. The   boys   _____ washroom is on the first floor.

5.   Susie   _____ brother is in the first grade.

6. That slice of pizza was   my   _____ .

Pronoun Agreement

D. Place the pronoun that agrees with the noun it replaces in the space provided.

1. John hit a home run. It was his / him _____ first big hit.

2. Paul and Jim bought they / their _____ shoes at the same store.

3. We were excited about us / our _____ first trip to Europe.

4. The teacher read a story from he / his _____ favourite book.

Adjectives and Adverbs

Adjectives can be formed by making changes to words. Some words can be changed to adverbs by adding "ly" to the ending.

E. Circle the adjective form in the following table.

1.	happiness	happy	2.	sadness	sad
3.	cooling	cold	4.	courage	courageous
5.	funny	fun	6.	terror	terrible
7.	danger	dangerous	8.	quick	quickness

F. Circle the adverb form in the following table.

1.	quick	quickly	2.	merrily	merry
3.	smooth	smoothly	4.	rounded	around
5.	nice	nicely	6.	creatively	creation
7.	mindfully	mind	8.	secure	securely

G. Put each group of words in a sensible order to make a simple sentence. Find the verb first. Look for a noun as the subject of the sentence.

1. season   is   our   longest   winter

    _____

2. get   seldom   dogs   along   cats   and

    _____

3. into   the   game   overtime   hockey   went

    _____

4. many   how   days   year   school   there   in   are   a

    _____

5. left   storm   everything   the   covered   snow   with

    _____

H. Match the subjects in Column A with suitable predicates in Column B.

Column A   Column B

1.   The students   A saved the man's life

2.   The figure skater   B listened to the teacher

3.   The doctor   C turned everyone upside down

4.   The roller coaster   D slipped and fell

Vowel Sounds

I.   Write "long" or "short" after each word to indicate the vowel sound.

1. fluke   _____   2. luck   _____

3.　truck　＿＿＿＿＿＿＿＿　　4.　made　＿＿＿＿＿＿＿＿

5.　ripe　＿＿＿＿＿＿＿＿　　6.　ate　＿＿＿＿＿＿＿＿

7.　eat　＿＿＿＿＿＿＿＿　　8.　pin　＿＿＿＿＿＿＿＿

9.　needle　＿＿＿＿＿＿＿＿　　10.　stone　＿＿＿＿＿＿＿＿

Digraphs

Digraphs are formed when two letters placed together make a single sound.

J.　Make a rhyming digraph from the following words.

1.　team　＿＿＿＿＿＿＿＿　　2.　beach　＿＿＿＿＿＿＿＿

3.　coat　＿＿＿＿＿＿＿＿　　4.　pail　＿＿＿＿＿＿＿＿

5.　pain　＿＿＿＿＿＿＿＿　　6.　stay　＿＿＿＿＿＿＿＿

7.　roast　＿＿＿＿＿＿＿＿　　8.　feet　＿＿＿＿＿＿＿＿

Consonants

A consonant is any letter that is not a vowel. A consonant blend is formed when two or more consonants placed together make a blended sound.

K.　Complete the words using the meanings given.

1. s l ＿＿ h	wet snow	2. ＿＿ e a m	thick milk
3. ＿ t r ＿＿ m	small river	4. c h ＿＿ k	write on the blackboard
5. ＿＿ i p	a holiday	6. s n ＿＿ k ＿	tricky, sly
7. s ＿ r ＿ p	useless piece	8. t e ＿＿＿ i b ＿ e	awful
9. t h ＿＿＿＿	toss	10. s w ＿ t	hit a fly

Are You Superstitious?

If you are a superstitious person, you probably believe in bad luck and will do certain things to prevent bad things from happening to you.

Did you know that walking under a ladder was bad luck? This superstition began many years ago when criminals were hanged in public. The ladder that led to the scaffold was a symbol of death. You may see someone knock on wood for good luck. Long ago, it was believed that gods lived in trees and if you knocked on the tree, the god would be happy and take care of you.

Breaking a mirror is supposed to mean seven years of bad luck. This idea came from the belief that the image in the mirror was actually a person's soul. If the mirror broke, the soul would be lost forever.

The day when people are most superstitious is Friday the 13th. The fact that Jesus Christ died on a Friday and that there were 13 men at the Last Supper could be reasons for this belief. Another might be that Friday was called "hangman's day", a day when criminals were executed.

Whether you are superstitious or not shouldn't matter as long as you keep your fingers crossed.

Recalling Details

A. Place "T" for true or "F" for false beside each statement.

1. Walking under a ladder is bad luck because something could fall on your head. .... ☐

2. Superstitious people believe in bad luck. .... ☐

3. Long ago, people believed that gods lived in trees. .... ☐

4. Knocking on wood would bring you good luck. .... ☐

5. Breaking a mirror may bring 20 years of bad luck. .... ☐

6. The most superstitious day is the 13th of each month. .... ☐

7. Friday was commonly known as "hangman's day". .... ☐

8. A person's soul was thought to be reflected in a mirror. .... ☐

9. Keeping your fingers crossed is supposed to bring good luck. .... ☐

10. Criminals were hanged on Friday. .... ☐

B. Here are some other well-known superstitions. Can you match them with the beliefs?

Superstition   Belief

1. (black cat   ○)   (A don't step on it)

2. (bless you   ○)   (B crossing your path brings bad luck)

3. (crack in the sidewalk ○)   (C say it after a person sneezes)

Types of Sentences

- Sentences are written for different purposes.

  1. An interrogative sentence asks a question.

     Example: What time is it? (A question mark follows an interrogative sentence.)

  2. A declarative sentence makes a simple statement.

     Example: The boy walked his dog. (A period ends a declarative sentence.)

  3. An exclamatory sentence shows emotion.

     Example: Look out for the car! (An exclamatory sentence is followed by an exclamation mark.)

  4. An imperative sentence tells what you want to happen.

     Example: Wait until you're called. (An imperative sentence is followed by a period.)

C. Punctuate each sentence, and state the type of sentence (interrogative, declarative, imperative, exclamatory) in the space provided.

At the Baseball Game

At a professional baseball game, exciting things happen.

1. Take your seats before the game begins _____

2. Which team is winning so far _____

3. The pitcher has struck out three batters _____

4. The bases are loaded _____

5. Wow, what a great catch _____

6. Is the runner fast enough to steal a base _____

D. Pretend you are at the game. Make up four sentences about the game, one for each type of sentence listed above.

1. Interrogative _____

2. Declarative _____

3. Imperative _____

4. Exclamatory _____

Compound Words

- A Compound Word is formed when two words are put together to form a word of a different meaning.

  Example: fire + place = fireplace

E. Match the words from Balloon A with those from Balloon B to make new words. Write your new words in the spaces below.

Use the clues to figure out the combinations.

A

basket	air
home	bed
snow	over
play	out
photo	night

B

room	flow
mare	ball
port	ground
work	man
graph	side

1. _____ a game

2. _____ school at home

3. _____ build one

4. _____ swings and things

5. _____ picture this

6. _____ land the jet

7. _____ nap time

8. _____ too full

9. _____ not in the house

10. _____ bad dream

 Challenge

It's a very spooky place.

F. Unscramble the compound word.

R A Y D + G E R A V = __ R __ __ E __ __ R __

Babies of the Arctic

Although the Arctic is a very cold place, there is a variety of wildlife that <u>inhabits</u> the area. The walrus, the seal, and the polar bear are the better-known Arctic animals. Their babies are wrapped in fur or fat to protect them from the bitter cold.

The walrus mother feeds her baby milk for two years. To protect their babies from polar bears and killer whales, walruses stay in groups. When danger <u>appears</u>, they form a circle with their

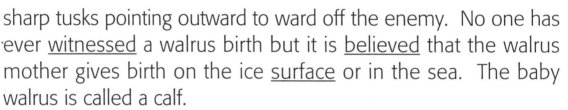

sharp tusks pointing outward to ward off the enemy. No one has ever <u>witnessed</u> a walrus birth but it is <u>believed</u> that the walrus mother gives birth on the ice <u>surface</u> or in the sea. The baby walrus is called a calf.

The seal is only a mother for ten days. Seals leave their pups to take care of themselves. At first, they cry for their mother. When they realize that she is not coming back, they dive into the sea. <u>Immediately</u> they learn how to swim and hunt for food.

Although a big meat-eater, the baby polar bear is born without teeth. The cub cannot see or hear at birth and cannot even walk for a month. Since the cubs do not have enough fur to protect them from the cold, the mother <u>smothers</u> them in her coat and feeds them warm milk. The mother bear must teach the cubs everything necessary for <u>survival</u>.

Remarkably, most of these Arctic babies survive the cold and the danger of <u>predators</u> and grow to <u>adulthood</u> adding to the Arctic animal population.

Recalling Details

A. Write short answers for the following questions. If necessary, look back over the story to find the answers.

1. How long does the walrus mother feed her babies?

   _____

2. Which Arctic animals are natural enemies of the baby walrus?

   _____

3. How do walruses ward off predators?

   _____

4. How long does the seal take care of her babies?

   _____

5. Why is the polar bear cub considered completely helpless at birth?

   _____

6. What does the mother polar bear do to keep her baby warm?

   _____

7. What natural protection do most Arctic babies have against the cold?

   _____

Your Opinion

B. Answer the question.

Three dangers that babies of the Arctic face are cold, lack of food, and predators. Which do you think is the worst of these dangers? Give a reason for your choice.

_____

_____

Plural Nouns

- To make a noun plural, usually you can simply add "s". However, some nouns require changes and different plural endings. Here are the rules of plural nouns.
  1. Single nouns – just add "s"
  2. Nouns ending in "s", "z", "ch", "sh", and "x" – add "es"
  3. Nouns ending in "y" – change the "y" to "i" and add "es"
  4. Nouns ending in "f" or "fe" – change the "f" to a "v" and add "es"
  5. Nouns ending in "o" – add either "s" or "es" (depending on the word)
  6. Some nouns stay the same.
  7. Some nouns change in the middle.

C. Circle the correct plural forms of the words and state which rules you are following by putting the numbers of the rules in the spaces provided.

No.	Word				
1.	ship	shipes	ships	shipies	rule #
2.	fox	foxes	foxen	foxs	
3.	wife	wifes	wives	wifies	
4.	knife	knives	knifes	knifies	
5.	potato	potatos	potatoes	potatose	
6.	goose	gooses	geeses	geese	
7.	tomato	tomatoes	tomatose	tomatos	
8.	boot	boots	beets	booties	
9.	foot	foots	feet	footies	
10.	half	halfs	halves	halfies	
11.	enemy	enemies	enemys	enemyies	
12.	key	keies	keyies	keys	
13.	ski	skis	skies	skys	
14.	sky	skies	skys	skyse	

New Words – Building Vocabulary

D. In "Babies of the Arctic", there are ten words underlined. Match the underlined words with the meanings.

Read the sentences in which these words appear and figure out their meanings.

Underlined Word

1. inhabits
2. appears
3. witnessed
4. believed
5. surface
6. immediately
7. smothers
8. survival
9. predators
10. adulthood

Meaning

A   right away

B   thought it was true

C   the top of something

D   go on living

E   covers completely

F   hunters

G   saw it happen

H   to live there

I   grown-ups

J   comes into view

E. Create new words from the underlined words. Change these words from the above list by adding new beginnings or endings.

1. survival   + ing   = _____

2. believed   + able   = _____

3. appears   + ance   = _____

4. inhabits   + un   = _____

The Origin of Gum Chewing

Next time your teacher tells you not to chew gum in class, you could say that you are exercising your jaw. That's the reason a dentist named William Semple invented gum in 1869. But his gum was not a big success because it was flavourless. People preferred to chew the gum from the spruce tree because it had a pleasant taste.

Spruce gum was scarce because spruce trees were being cut down to make paper. A man by the name of Thomas Adams came across chicle, a rubbery sap from the sapodilla tree of South America. He combined chicle with gum to create a new flavour sensation. In 1871, Adams invented a machine that made chicle gum into sticks. He claimed that his gum could improve blood circulation, strengthen teeth, and refresh the brain.

Soon, candy-coated gum named "little chicles" came along, which became known as "Chiclets". Following the invention of Chiclets was Blibber-Blubber. It was a strong form of gum that enabled the chewer to blow bubbles. Soon, people around the world started chewing gum.

Further traces of the history of gum might be found underneath your desk. For years, students have been hiding their gum there to prevent being caught chewing gum in class. An even quicker way of getting rid of the evidence is to do what millions of school children have done over the years – swallow it. This may make the gum disappear quickly but it is not a good idea because gum never really gets digested properly.

Comprehension Crossword Puzzle

A. Solve the crossword puzzle using words from the story, "The Origin of Gum Chewing".

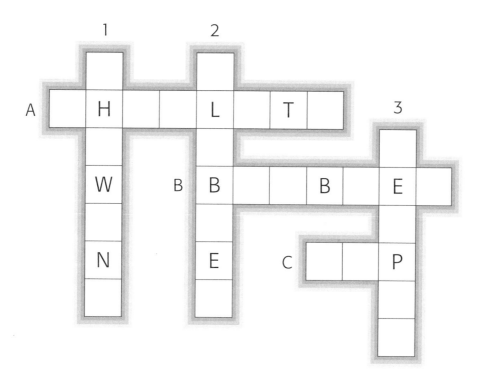

Across

A. candy-coated gum
B. what you can blow
C. chicle is a rubbery form of this

Down

1. exercising with gum
2. goes with Blubber
3. William's other name

Your Opinion

B. Give two reasons why you think chewing gum is so popular throughout the world.

1. _____

2. _____

Verb Tenses – Past, Present, and Future

- *Verbs change according to which time period they are in.*

  Examples: *I walk. I am walking. – present time*

  I walked. I did walk. I was walking. I have walked. – past time

  I will walk. I shall walk. – future time

C. Write the missing verb tenses in the chart below.

	Present	Past	Future
1.	carry		
2.		ran	
3.	think		
4.			will fight
5.	try		
6.			will swim

D. Fill in the blanks with the proper forms of the verbs in parentheses.

1. Jim (play) _____ basketball yesterday.

2. Susan (try) _____ to help you tomorrow.

3. The students (work) _____ on their projects for two days.

4. Paul and Peter (fly) _____ the kite when the wind comes up.

5. She (walk) _____ home with her friends every day.

6. His parents (take) _____ a holiday next summer.

7. He usually (go) _____ shopping on weekends.

8. I (meet) _____ Jason this morning on my way to school.

Homophones

- Homophones are words that sound the same but are spelled differently.

  Example: hear   here
            I could not <u>hear</u> what he said.   He was <u>here</u> on time.

E. Read each sentence and select the proper homophone to suit the meaning.

Use a dictionary if you are not sure which word to use.

1. He has bean / been _____ to school every day.

2. My father / farther _____ works downtown.

3. I would / wood _____ like to travel.

4. When she was ill, she looked pale / pail _____ .

5. All weak / week _____ we have to go to school.

6. The hair / hare _____ beat the tortoise in a race.

7. I couldn't stop my bicycle because the brake / break _____ didn't work.

8. The cake was made out of flower / flour _____ .

9. The made / maid _____ cleaned the hotel room.

10. We had to weight / wait _____ in line.

11. The turtle fell into the hole / whole _____ .

12. You shoud write / right _____ the answer in the box.

Trick or Treat

On Halloween Night, children go trick-or-treating in their neighbourhoods. Dressed up as ghosts, skeletons, devils, and various other characters, children knock on doors to collect their treats. Seldom do they actually perform a "trick".

It is thought that trick-or-treating comes from an old English custom. On All Souls Day, poor people went begging and promised to say prayers in exchange for food. Apple bobbing, still a favourite Halloween game, was originally an ancient ceremony honouring harvest time.

A jack-o'-lantern is placed on porches and windows to tell children that treats are available. The legend has it that a man named Jack couldn't enter heaven because he played tricks on the devil. As punishment, he had to wander the earth carrying a lantern waiting to be judged fit to get into heaven.

People believed that Halloween marked the connection between the world of the living and the world of the dead. This meant that ghosts would roam the earth on this night. Some believed that these ghosts would go back to the homes they lived in before they died.

Thankfully, Halloween is a fun night where children can dress up and get a bag full of candy. We don't have to worry about ghosts. Or do we?

Matching Facts

A. **Match the facts from Column A with the meanings in Column B.**

Column A

1. trick-or-treating

2. apple bobbing

3. jack-o'-lantern

4. Jack

5. All Souls Day

Column B

A shows that treats are available

B old English custom

C people went begging

D honours harvest time

E wanders the earth

Happy Halloween!

B. **Write a short answer for each question.**

1. Why did Jack have to wander the earth?

_____

_____

2. Why did ghosts roam the earth at Halloween?

_____

_____

3. How do children know where they can collect treats?

_____

_____

Contractions

- Contractions are single words that are formed by combining and shortening two words.

  Examples: can + not = cannot ⟶ can't

  I + will = I'll

  Note the use of the apostrophe to replace letters.

C. Form contractions from the following pairs of words.

1. she will = _____
2. he had = _____
3. we are = _____
4. you are = _____
5. were not = _____
6. who is = _____
7. did not = _____
8. has not = _____
9. I am = _____
10. that is = _____
11. have not = _____
12. would not = _____
13. is not = _____
14. there is = _____

Be Creative

You may write about Halloween.

D. Use five of the contractions to make sentences of your own.

1. _____
2. _____
3. _____
4. _____
5. _____

Halloween Words

E. **Here are some familiar Halloween words. Write a Halloween story using some of these words.**

You might want to tell of a scary Halloween night that you remember. Draw a picture of your favourite Halloween costume in the box. Draw other pictures that create a Halloween mood.

ghosts	scary	windy	shadows	noises	candy
skeletons	graveyard	dark	witches	bats	moon
pumpkin	screams	chills	costumes	goblins	masks

Understanding the Food Chain

The simple garden shows how a food chain works. Suppose you have lettuce growing in your garden. That lettuce gets energy from sunlight. It also soaks up water and nutrients from the soil. It now has everything it needs to grow. Think of this lettuce as the first link in a garden food chain.

Suppose one night a slug slithers onto the leaf of the lettuce and begins eating it. The energy from the lettuce is now transferred to the slug. The slug becomes the second link in the food chain. In the morning, a beetle comes along and eats the slug. The energy from the slug is now passed on to the beetle, which becomes the third link in the chain.

Just then, along comes a hungry shrew that eats the beetle. Now the shrew is enjoying all the energy in the chain. But the food chain is not over. A wise old owl swoops down, picks up the shrew, and returns to its nest to prepare it for dinner.

The owl has no natural predators. That means that there is no animal that tries to kill the owl for food. The owl is at the top of this food chain and benefits from all the energy passed through all the members of the chain – the lettuce, the slug, the beetle, and the shrew.

There are many different food chains in nature. Each environment has its own food chain. We, too, are part of a food chain. Lucky for us, like the wise old owl, we are also at the top of our chain.

Understanding Facts

A. Put the members of this food chain in order.

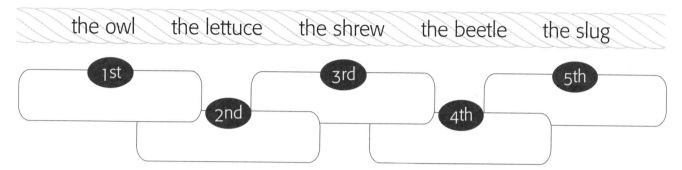

the owl   the lettuce   the shrew   the beetle   the slug

1st

2nd

3rd

4th

5th

Understanding Information

B. Answer the following questions about the food chain.

1. In the food chain, what is the role of the sun and the nutrients in the soil?

_____

_____

2. What does it mean to transfer energy?

_____

_____

3. Why do you think that the owl has no natural predators?

_____

_____

4. If we are part of a food chain, what position in the chain would we be placed?

_____

5. Can you name three animals that would be at the top of their food chains? (not from the reading passage)

A. _____   B. _____   C. _____

Capitalization

- Here are some rules of capitalization:
    1. Use a capital letter to begin a sentence.
    2. Use a capital letter for names (people, pets).
    3. Use a capital for the names of places on the map (cities, lakes, rivers, countries...).
    4. Use a capital for names of places and things such as buildings, companies, and historic sights.
    5. Use a capital for days of the week and months of the year.
    6. Use a capital for titles (Dr., Mr., Mrs., Miss, Ms., Prime Minister, President, Professor, Prince, Queen...).
    7. Use capitals for the words in titles of books, movies, and songs (even your own stories).

C. **There are 33 missing capitals in the story below. Write over the letters that should be capitalized in dark pen or pencil.**

You be the teacher. Correct the work.

my trip to england

my name is billy henderson. i live at 723 main st. my dad is a doctor and his patients call him dr. henderson. this summer we are going on a holiday to england to visit my aunt, rita. rita lives near the thames river. we are going to visit buckingham palace while we are there. our flight is booked on british airways and we will land at heathrow airport. we are leaving on august 11 and returning on september 3. while we are away, our neighbour, mrs. watson, will look after our dog, scamp.

Synonyms

- A Synonym is a word that means the same as another word.

D. Complete the crossword puzzle with words that match the clues.

Try to match the synonyms in the word bank to the clue words first.

plate   stay   end   saw

unhappy   drop   nasty   add   seas

Across

A. sad

B. oceans

C. total

D. remain

E. finish

Down

1. cut

2. rude

3. dish

4. lower

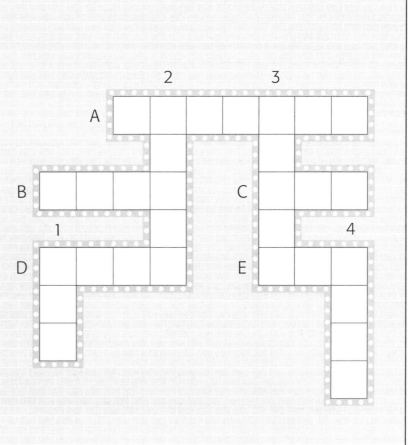

The Biggest Pest of the Summer

Most people would agree that summer's biggest pest is the mosquito. This pesky little insect can quickly ruin a walk in the woods or a holiday at a cottage.

Actually, only the female mosquito bites. The male mosquito feeds on plant juices. The female mosquito drinks our blood to get protein needed to make eggs. One bite into your arm or leg can help the female mosquito produce 50 to 100 eggs.

The mosquito has a pointed beak that sticks into your skin. Once your skin is pierced, the mosquito spits saliva into the wound to stop the blood from clotting. When the blood is prevented from clotting, it is easier for the mosquito to fill up on your blood. The saliva causes your skin to itch and swell up.

Some people attract mosquitoes more than others. To prevent mosquitoes from biting you, there are some things you can do. Avoid wearing dark colours and clothes made of rough materials. Blue jeans, for example, will attract mosquitoes. Don't wear perfume or use shampoo. These scents attract these annoying insects. Probably the best prevention is a good insect repellent.

Mosquitoes are very sneaky. They land without a sound and weigh almost nothing. You usually notice them only after they have already enjoyed a meal of your blood.

Checking Facts

There are 5 true answers.

A.   Place "T" for true and "F" for false in the space provided beside each statement.

1.   Only the male mosquito bites people. .... ☐

2.   Mosquitoes spit saliva into the wound from the bite. .... ☐

3.   The saliva in the wound stops blood from clotting. .... ☐

4.   There is seldom an itch after a bite. .... ☐

5.   The mosquito's saliva can stop bleeding. .... ☐

6.   All people attract mosquitoes the same. .... ☐

7.   Light coloured clothes attract mosquitoes. .... ☐

8.   Blue jeans attract mosquitoes. .... ☐

9.   Mosquitoes do not like perfume and shampoo. .... ☐

10.   Mosquitoes are noisy. .... ☐

11.   Mosquitoes are very light. .... ☐

12.   One mosquito can produce 50 to 100 eggs. .... ☐

Using Information

B.   Answer the questions.

1.   Imagine you are at a cottage in the middle of mosquito season. What would you do to protect yourself?

   _____

   _____

2.   Explain how the mosquito sucks blood.

   _____

   _____

Noun and Verb Agreement

- When you write a sentence, it is important to have the noun (subject) agree with the verb (predicate).

- If the subject is singular, the verb must be singular.
  If the subject is plural, the verb must be plural.

C. Write the proper verb in each of the sentences below.

1. Jim and Jackie (is, are) _____ cousins.

2. Paul (are, is) _____ leaving early.

3. The students will (comes, come) _____ to the gym.

4. The animals in the forest (was, were) _____ restless.

5. Good weather (are, is) _____ important when on holiday.

6. Travelling on foot (were, was) _____ tiring.

7. John and Paul have (took, taken) _____ the bus.

8. Susie, Janice, and Brenda (like, likes) _____ soft ice cream.

Tricky Situations

- 1. Words such as "anyone", "each", "everyone", and "no one" always use singular verbs.

  2. If the subject is a group such as "teammates" or "members", then use a verb that agrees with the noun.

  3. Single words that refer to groups (family, school, team) usually have singular verbs.

D. Pick the correct verb forms to suit these tricky nouns.

1. The team will (arrives, arrive) _____ today.

2. The members of the club (is, are) _____ having a meeting.

3. Everyone (is, are) _____ coming to the party.

4. Each of the boys (comes, come) _____ by car.

5. Anyone (is, are) _____ welcome to join the group.

6. The schools (was, were) _____ getting together to raise money.

Antonyms

- An Antonym is a word that has the opposite meaning of another word.

E. Solve the antonym word puzzles. Unscramble the antonyms and place the answers in the boxes.

#	Scramble	Boxes	Clue
1.	m e n y e		friend
2.	l a y p		work
3.	e f a s		dangerous
4.	d r a h		soft
5.	m a c l		windy
6.	u n i r		repair
7.	p m e y t		crowded

F. Circle the antonym for each word from the choices.

#	Word		Choices		
1.	beautiful	ugly	happy	careful	pretty
2.	funny	joking	comical	serious	laughing
3.	unusual	regular	peculiar	odd	strange
4.	exciting	interesting	dull	fun	scary
5.	tame	soft	gentle	wild	rare
6.	strong	tough	rough	weak	heavy

The Mystery of Migration

Before winter arrives, many species of birds instinctively know that it's time to head south. The mystery of migration has always puzzled us. Why do only some birds migrate? How do birds know when to go south? How do they find their way?

Some birds fly south because their food supply runs short in winter. The woodpecker, for example, does not need to fly south because it can find food stuck in the bark of trees. The insects that the woodpecker eats are safe in the bark from the winter cold and snow.

Some birds rely on grains, shoots, insects, and other foods that disappear in winter. These birds must head south where food is still available. But why do they not stay south? Perhaps they know that if they stayed down south, they would run out of food there, too.

It is possible that birds know when winter is coming because they notice that the days are getting shorter. Once they leave from the north, they use the sun as a compass. The sun is in different positions in the sky at various times of day. In order to use it as a guide, birds would have to know the time of day. On long flights, birds use the stars to navigate their route.

The homing pigeon does not use the sun or the stars. Scientists believe that it uses the magnetic field of the earth. One of the most amazing migrations is that of the tiny hummingbird. It travels from Canada to Mexico – a distance of over 3,200 kilometres.

Choosing Correct Facts

A. Place a check mark in the space beside the correct answer that matches each statement.

1. Birds know when to fly south because
    A. they see the sunrise. .... ☐
    B. they have good instincts. .... ☐
    C. they follow a leader. .... ☐

2. It is believed that birds fly south because
    A. they need food. .... ☐
    B. they like warm weather. .... ☐
    C. they get lost. .... ☐

3. The woodpecker does not need to fly south because
    A. it has no instincts. .... ☐
    B. its food is protected in the bark of trees. .... ☐
    C. it does not know the way. .... ☐

4. Birds do not stay south because
    A. they get too warm. .... ☐
    B. they follow the sun. .... ☐
    C. they do not want the food supply to run out down south. ...... ☐

5. On long migration flights, birds navigate by
    A. the stars. .... ☐
    B. other birds. .... ☐
    C. the weather. .... ☐

6. The homing pigeon is different because it finds its way by
    A. following the sun. .... ☐
    B. using the magnetic field of the earth. .... ☐
    C. following the same route. .... ☐

Building Sentences with Adverbs and Adjectives

- Remember that an Adjective describes a noun and an Adverb describes a verb. We use adjectives and adverbs to give more information and make sentences more interesting.

B. Rewrite the following sentences and add both the adjectives and adverbs in parentheses.

1. The boy ran. (happy, quickly)

   _____

2. The wind blew. (howling, furiously)

   _____

3. The grade three students sang the songs. (talented, loudly)

   _____

4. The game was finished. (exciting, early)

   _____

5. John, the boy in the class, was late. (oldest, again)

   _____

C. Add your own descriptive words to the story below.

The 1._____ girl received a 2._____ bicycle for her birthday. She was very 3._____ to get such a 4._____ gift. She rode 5._____ down the road towards the 6._____ house of her 7._____ friend, Sarah. It was a very 8._____ day for her.

Idioms

- *"Don't have a cow, man."* ...Bart Simpson

- *An Idiom is a group of words that has a meaning other than what it really means. Rather, an idiom has another meaning that makes sense if you know the origin or the real message behind the words.*

- *We use idioms today to get ideas across. Idioms are convenient because they are widely known and understood.*

D. Here are some everyday idioms. Can you guess what they mean? Write explanations in the spaces provided.

1. He led me on a *wild goose chase*.

   _____

2. *The early bird catches the worm.*

   _____

3. We tried to *butter up* the teacher to get less homework.

   _____

4. When she lost her cat, she was *feeling blue*.

   _____

5. The grade three students were *in hot water* over the broken window.

   _____

6. My dad *blew his top* when he got a flat tire.

   _____

E. Write sentences using these other idioms.

1. out of this world _____

2. spill the beans _____

3. going bananas _____

Mary Kate and Ashley Olsen

The twin sisters, Mary Kate and Ashley Olsen, are two of the most popular television, film, and music stars in North America. And, they are only fourteen years old! When they were younger, they were already famous. Recently, they have returned to television to star in their own show, "Two of a Kind".

The twins were born on July 13, 1986. They live in Los Angeles, California with their family. They have a brother named Trent and a sister named Elizabeth. Both Trent and Elizabeth sometimes appear in their videos.

From the age of 9 months until the age of 9 years, they both played the role of Michelle Tanner on the hit series, "Full House". They not only starred in television, they made home videos and party tapes as well. The "Our First Video" production of theirs was No. 1 on the Billboard chart and remained on top for 12 weeks. It stayed in the top 10 for 157 weeks. All this was accomplished when they were only 7 years old!

Mary Kate and Ashley, although famous, are very ordinary children. They like to shop, sing and act, dance, and watch music videos. Even though they have earned a lot of money from starring on television, they only receive $10.00 a week allowance.

Each month, the twins get thousands of letters from fans. Their official fan club is called: Mary Kate & Ashley Fan Club. The address is 859 Hollywood Way, Suite 412, Burbank, CA, 91505.

Remembering Details

A. Fill in the blanks.

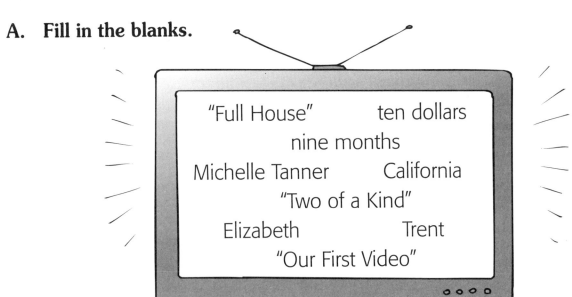

"Full House"   ten dollars
nine months
Michelle Tanner   California
"Two of a Kind"
Elizabeth   Trent
"Our First Video"

1. Mary Kate and Ashley starred in a television show when they were

   _____ old.

2. Recently they have starred in the show _____ .

3. When they were young, they shared the role of _____

   in their first television show.

4. Their first television show was called _____ .

5. Their No. 1 video was called _____ .

6. The twin sisters have earned a lot of money in television but they only

   get _____ a week allowance.

7. They have a brother named _____ and a sister named

   _____ .

8. Their fan club is in the state of _____ .

Letter Writing

B. Write a letter to Mary Kate and Ashley Olsen.

Think of 3 or 4 questions you might ask them. Try to write complete sentences with descriptive words. Tell them something about you: where you live, your family members, the name of your school, your hobbies, your pet's name.

Date: _____

Dear Mary Kate and Ashley,

_____

_____

All about
yourself here → _____

_____

_____

_____

_____

Ask questions
about them ✎ _____
here

_____

_____

_____

Closing remark ↗ _____

Yours truly,

Your name: _____

Building New Words

- *New Words are built from root words.*

  Example: true ——→ *untrue truly truth*

C. Find the words in the word search.

B	U	I	L	D	I	N	G	J	K
H	A	R	M	F	U	L	Q	W	E
A	S	M	P	I	T	I	F	U	L
P	A	F	T	N	E	W	E	S	T
P	R	I	C	E	L	E	S	S	R
I	R	T	O	S	S	I	N	G	A
N	O	N	H	T	R	V	U	L	P
E	V	E	N	T	F	U	L	Z	P
S	E	S	A	D	N	E	S	S	E
S	N	S	T	O	P	P	E	R	D

happiness   harmful   finest   newest

pitiful   priceless   eventful   trapped

tossing   sadness   stopper   building

D. Write out the root word of each of these words.

1.	2.	3.
4.	5.	6.
7.	8.	9.
10.	11.	12.

Multiple Choice

A. Underline the best completion for each sentence.

1. The ladder that led to the hanging scaffold was a symbol of
   A. bad luck.   B. death.   C. good luck.

2. Breaking a mirror means seven years of
   A. hard times.   B. being poor.   C. hard luck.

3. People are most superstitious on
   A. Friday the 13th.   B. Halloween.   C. New Year's Eve.

4. Many Arctic baby animals are kept warm by
   A. fire.   B. the sun.   C. fur or fat.

5. A seal baby is called a
   A. calf.   B. pup.   C. cub.

6. At first, gum was not a big success because it was
   A. too sticky.   B. flavourless.   C. too rubbery.

7. In 1871 Adams invented a machine to turn gum into
   A. candy.   B. bubble gum.   C. sticks.

8. Trick-or-treating is an old custom from
   A. England.   B. Spain.   C. Germany.

9. Today, a jack-o'-lantern on a porch means that
   A. candy is available. B. beware of ghosts. C. nobody's home.

10. In the old days, on All Souls Day poor people went
    A. trick-or-treating. B. begging for food. C. to Church.

11. The last link in a food chain has no
   A. way to get food.　B. natural enemies.　C. growth.

12. The male mosquito feeds on
   A. human blood.　　B. other mosquitoes.　C. plant juices.

13. The saliva placed in the bite by the mosquito prevents
   A. blood clotting.　　B. itching.　　　　C. swelling.

14. To avoid being bitten by a mosquito, avoid wearing
   A. dark colours.　　B. light colours.　　C. colourful clothing.

15. A female mosquito can lay up to
   A. 1,000 eggs.　　B. 100 eggs.　　　C. 500 eggs.

16. To know when to head south, birds rely on
   A. other birds.　　B. their memory.　　C. instinct.

17. The woodpecker does not have to fly south because
   A. its food is protected in a tree.　B. it doesn't get cold.
   C. it has no instincts.

18. The homing pigeon is probably guided by
   A. the sounds of other birds.　　B. the magnetic field of the earth.
   C. the stars.

19. From the age of 9 months to 9 years, Mary Kate and Ashley starred in the television show
   A. "Empty Place".　B. "Full House".　　C. "Our House".

20. Mary Kate and Ashley live in
   A. Kansas City.　　B. New York City.　　C. Los Angeles.

21. Mary Kate and Ashley were born in
   A. 1986.　　　B. 1990.　　　　C. 1980.

Capitalization

B. In the following sentences, place capital letters over the small letters that should be capitalized.

1. mr. jones was also known as dr. jones when he was at toronto general hospital.

2. linda and lauren attended willow avenue public school.

3. they took a canoe trip on the niagara river near quebec city.

4. we all read the harry potter books by j.k. rowling.

Plural Nouns

C. Write the plural forms of the following nouns.

1.	ship		2.	potato	
3.	foot		4.	knife	
5.	fox		6.	half	
7.	wife		8.	ski	

Types of Sentences

D. Place the name of the type of sentence (declarative, interrogative, imperative, exclamatory) in each space below. Punctuate each sentence.

1. How are you feeling today _____

2. Today is Monday _____

3. Look out _____

4. Sit down and be quiet _____

Contractions

E. Change the following words to contraction form.

1.	she will		2.	we will	
3.	did not		4.	have not	
5.	would not		6.	that is	

Verb Tenses

F. Change the verb tenses to suit the sense of the sentences.

1. He (arrive) _____ home tomorrow.

2. I (walk) _____ a long way yesterday.

3. The dog (jump) _____ over the fence when his master commands.

4. The men (work) _____ on the bridge all of last week.

Noun and Verb Agreement

G. Place the correct forms of the verbs in the spaces provided.

1. John and Phillip (is, are) _____ in the same class.

2. We (were, was) _____ happy to see them.

3. The children (go, goes) _____ to their classrooms.

4. They (take, takes) _____ a break for lunch.

5. Fish (are, is) _____ swimming in the aquarium.

Synonyms

H. In each group, underline the word that is **not** a synonym for the one on the left.

Synonyms are words that mean the same as other words.

1.	unhappy	miserable	joyous	upset
2.	creative	smart	dull	imaginative
3.	swift	quick	fast	sluggish
4.	large	huge	massive	tiny
5.	loud	noisy	thunderous	silent
6.	powerful	weak	strong	muscular
7.	careful	careless	cautious	attentive

Antonyms

I. In each group, underline the word that **is** an antonym for the one on the left.

Antonyms are words that are opposite of other words.

1.	friendly	nice	happy	rude
2.	crowded	empty	populated	full
3.	rough	smooth	plain	rugged
4.	wet	soaked	dry	drenched
5.	plump	skinny	muscular	chubby
6.	shiny	silvery	dull	cold
7.	hurt	injured	wounded	healthy

Compound Words

J. Match the words that make good compound word combinations. Write the compound words.

Group A

fire	straw	photo
base	bath	fore
hand	note	pillow
grape	out	down
every	mail	

Group B

room	ball	place
head	writing	berry
graph	fruit	book
town	one	box
side	case	

1. _____   2. _____   3. _____

4. _____   5. _____   6. _____

7. _____   8. _____   9. _____

10. _____   11. _____   12. _____

13. _____   14. _____

New Words

K. Match the new words with the definitions.

1.	inhabits		A	hunters
2.	witnessed		B	instantly
3.	predators		C	grown up
4.	immediately		D	saw it happen
5.	adulthood		E	lives in

Grammar

1 Nouns

A. Look at the picture. Colour the objects that are nouns. Write six of the nouns next to the picture.

1. _____

2. _____

3. _____

4. _____

5. _____

6. _____

B. Draw something you like to use at the playground.

Noun Groups / Families

C. Choose the noun that belongs with the group.

| Numbers | Animals | Colours | Mouth | Head | Fruits |

1.

apples
pears
bananas
pineapples
oranges

2.

eyes
nose
eyebrows
ears
cheeks

3.

teeth
tongue
lips
tonsils
gums

4.

tiger
lion
monkey
peacock
panda

5.

blue
orange
green
red
pink

6.

16
21
32
101
263

D. Fill in the missing letters to make new nouns.

1.
a. _c_ at
b. ___ at
c. ___ at
d. ___ at
e. ___ at

2.
a. _b_ and
b. ___ and
c. ___ and
d. ___ and
e. ___ and

3.
a. _d_ rain
b. ___ rain
c. ___ rain
d. ___ rain

Common Nouns

A common noun names any person, place, or thing.
Common nouns begin with lower case letters if they are not at the beginning of sentences.

E. Underline the common nouns in the sentences.

1. The girls are having a party.
2. The cars are in the parking lot.
3. They took the chess set out of the box.
4. She put on her new jacket.
5. The candle burned for hours.

F. Write the common noun beside each proper noun. Choose from the word bank.

> painting   supermarket   boy   mountain
> drug store   city   stadium

1. Mount Fuji   _____
2. SkyDome   _____
3. Toronto   _____
4. Shoppers Drug Mart _____
5. Dominion   _____
6. Mona Lisa   _____
7. Ryan   _____

Proper Nouns

 A proper noun names a specific person, place, or thing. Proper nouns begin with capitals.

G. Read the sentences. Underline the proper nouns.

1. Jennifer read her books.

2. The CN Tower is in Toronto.

3. The Parliament Buildings are in Ottawa.

4. Teddy is going to Bellriver School.

5. The panda comes from China.

6. Do you like the songs by the Spice Girls?

7. Tokyo is the capital city of Japan.

8. Have you ever been to Disneyland?

H. Read the common nouns. Write proper nouns to match.

1. street _____

2. school _____

3. boy _____

4. girl _____

5. shopping mall _____

6. store _____

7. city _____

8. country _____

9. river _____

2 Noun Plurals

Plural Nouns

A plural noun names more than one person, place, or thing.

Examples: ear → **ears**   trip → **trips**

To make a simple plural, you just add "s".

A. **Look at the picture. Count the things and write the numbers and the common nouns.**

1. __1__ __flag__   2. __ _____   3. __ _____

4. __ _____   5. __ _____   6. __ _____

7. __ _____   8. __ _____   9. __ _____

Most nouns are made plural by adding "s".

Some others are made plural by adding "es". Often, they are nouns ending in "s", "x", "ch", or "sh".

Examples: box → box**es**

bench → bench**es**

B. Match the singular with its plural noun. Draw a line from one to the other.

1. tax	lunches
2. wish	foxes
3. church	inches
4. bus	dishes
5. bush	churches
6. dish	ashes
7. inch	dresses
8. dress	wishes
9. peach	taxes
10. ash	bushes
11. lunch	peaches
12. fox	buses

Some nouns end in "y". In order to make them plural, you must drop the "y" and add "ies".

Example: party → part**ies**

C.   Write the plural nouns.

Singular	Plural	Singular	Plural
1. city	_____	2. bunny	_____
3. baby	_____	4. body	_____
5. lady	_____	6. country	_____
7. story	_____	8. factory	_____
9. family	_____	10. candy	_____

D.   Fill in the blanks with the plural nouns in (C).

1. The _____ are about toys.

2. Their _____ are going on a trip.

3. The _____ were hopping everywhere.

4. There were many _____ crawling.

5. Their _____ are strong and muscular.

6. There are many _____ in our province.

7. They gave the children some _____ .

8. The _____ had many workers.

Noun Review

Nouns name people, places, and things. Some nouns are made plural (more than one) by adding "s", "es", or "ies".

E.   Read the clues. Count the spaces for letters. Fill in the blanks.

1. You wear me on your feet. One of me is a _ _ _ _; two of me is a pair of _ _ _ _ _.

2. I have some chocolate chips in me. Eat one and it's a _ _ _ _ _ _ _; more than one are _ _ _ _ _ _ _ _.

3. You visit me when you are sick. I am a _ _ _ _ _ _ _ _. A hospital has many _ _ _ _ _ _ _ _ in it.

4. You can drink from me but I'll break if you drop me. One of me is a _ _ _ _ _ but more are _ _ _ _ _ _ _ _.

5. I buzz and carry pollen from flower to flower. If you see one of me, it's a _ _ _ _. Many _ _ _ _ _ make a swarm.

6. I am a person who is your mother's brother. If you have one, I'm an _ _ _ _ _; two are _ _ _ _ _ _ _.

7. When you make a _ _ _ _ on a star, dreams come true. In a lifetime, you can make a lot of _ _ _ _ _ _ _.

8. Some children ride one to school. It's a _ _ _ _. Every day, many _ _ _ _ _ _ drop children at school.

3 Irregular Plural Nouns

Most nouns are made plural by adding "s" or "es".

Some nouns have "irregular" plurals. The noun may stay the same or the plural may have some of the same letters as the singular form.

Examples: moose → **moose**   goose → **geese**

A. Read the words in Column A and Column B. Draw a line from each singular form to its plural form.

Column A (Singular)	Column B (Plural)
1. tooth	oxen
2. child	men
3. deer	salmon
4. salmon	children
5. woman	women
6. reindeer	feet
7. sheep	reindeer
8. man	teeth
9. foot	sheep
10. ox	deer

Some nouns are made plural by changing the ending "f" or "fe" to "ves".

Example: wife → wi**ves**

B. **Read each of the following sentences. Fill in the plural form for the singular noun given.**

1. The farmers' _____ (wife) all went to the new restaurant.

2. The _____ (calf) are running around the pasture.

3. The _____ (wolf) ran across the road.

4. The _____ (leaf) are changing colour.

5. There are some _____ (knife) in the kitchen.

6. Mommy cut the apple into _____ (half).

7. Be careful! Don't cut _____ (yourself).

8. Don't put too many books on the _____ (shelf).

9. The brave man saved the children's _____ (life).

10. The _____ (elf) liked wearing pointy shoes on their feet.

C. Read the nouns in the word bank. Circle the singular form in Word Search A. Circle the plural form in Word Search B. Write the noun pairs on the lines below.

Word Bank

wife   dice   lives   wives   scarf
scarves   knife   dice
life   rhinoceros   medium   rhinoceros
mouse   media   mice   knives

Word Search A

t	u	p	r	q	x	f	m
o	k	g	h	y	m	t	s
j	m	d	i	c	e	j	l
x	f	r	n	h	d	p	f
b	j	l	o	l	i	k	c
t	k	i	c	b	u	n	v
w	i	f	e	g	m	i	p
f	c	e	r	d	w	f	s
h	r	m	o	u	s	e	k
d	n	v	s	c	a	r	f

Word Search B

j	d	g	m	l	b	r	p
w	i	v	e	s	r	h	f
f	c	q	d	k	t	i	z
k	e	s	i	c	h	n	x
n	k	c	a	w	j	o	d
i	b	a	g	m	q	c	r
v	n	r	l	i	v	e	s
e	d	v	f	c	s	r	y
s	h	e	w	e	u	o	g
c	r	s	l	p	f	s	v

1. _____ _____   2. _____ _____

3. _____ _____   4. _____ _____

5. _____ _____   6. _____ _____

7. _____ _____   8. _____ _____

Irregular noun plurals are plurals that may have some of the same letters as the singular form. Some plurals use the same words as the singular.

D. Read the previous pages of irregular plurals. Find the correct plural to substitute for the singular.

1. There are many _____ (rhinoceros) at the zoo.

2. The prince saved all the people's _____ (life).

3. The tiny _____ (mouse) ran into the kitchen.

4. The numbers on the _____ (dice) showed 11.

5. All the _____ (sheep) were sheared for their wool.

6. There were several sharp _____ (knife) in the drawer.

7. King Henry VIII had many _____ (wife).

8. _____ (child) can feed the _____ (deer) here.

9. You stepped on my _____ (foot).

4 Pronouns and Articles

Subject Pronouns

 A pronoun is a word that takes the place of a noun.
Some subject pronouns are **I**, **he**, **she**, **it**, **we**, or **they**.

A. Read the first sentence. Fill in a pronoun for the underlined words.

1. <u>Jason and Sam</u> play together every day.

    _____ play together every day.

2. <u>Stephen</u> won the radio.

    _____ won the radio.

3. <u>My sister and I</u> like to sing.

    _____ like to sing.

B. Fill in the blanks with pronouns.

𝓜𝓪𝓴𝓲𝓷𝓰 Muffins

My mom is the best cook. 1._____ bakes great blueberry muffins. 2._____ have lots of blueberries. 3._____ put on our aprons before we start. Mom says 4._____ must turn the oven on so that 5._____ will be hot enough for baking. 6._____ bake the muffins for 20

minutes. 7._____ taste them. Yum. Yum. Good! Mom
keeps two for Dad. 8._____ likes muffins, too.

Object Pronouns

Pronouns take the place of nouns in sentences.
Object pronouns usually go at the end. Some object pronouns are **me**,
him, **her**, **it**, **us**, and **them**.

C. Rewrite the sentences using pronouns for the underlined nouns.

1. The bus is picking <u>Olivia and Julie</u> up at the station.

    _____

2. Michael can go to the movies with <u>Julie</u>.

    _____

3. Patricia is taking <u>the book</u> to <u>Dad</u>.

    _____

4. Mom has given <u>Janice and me</u> some chocolate.

    _____

D. Fill in the blanks in the newscast with pronouns.

> A hurricane named Sarah will hit
> 1._____ tomorrow. 2._____ will be
> touching down near 3._____ in the
> evening. 4._____ winds will get up to
> 100 km per hour.

Articles

"A", "an", and "the" are articles. They help nouns.

"A" is used before a noun that begins with a consonant.

"An" is used before a noun that begins with a vowel.

"The" is used before a particular person, place, or thing.

Examples: **a** coat   **an** ice cube   **the** park near my home

E.   Fill in the blanks with correct articles.

a   an

1. _____ tracksuit   2. _____ Inukshuk

3. _____ ox   4. _____ building

5. _____ store   6. _____ alphabet letter

7. _____ apple   8. _____ blueberry

9. _____ ski   10. _____ palm tree

F.   Use "a", "an", or "the" in the sentences below.

1. _____ square is _____ shape with four equal sides.

2. _____ octagon has eight sides.

3. _____ famous five-sided building in Washington is called _____ Pentagon.

4. _____ hexagon is _____ six-sided figure.

5. _____ oval is _____ shape that looks like _____ flat circle.

6. _____ rectangle has opposite sides that are equal.

Article and Pronoun Review

A pronoun is a word used in place of a noun. Some pronouns are "I", "you", "he", "she", "him", "her", "they", and "we". An article helps a noun. "A", "an", and "the" are articles.

G. Read the story. Choose the correct pronouns and articles. Fill in the blanks.

A penguin is 1._____ (a, the) bird that cannot fly. 2._____ (It, He) lives in Antarctica and in 3._____ (an, the) areas south of Australia and 4._____ (a, the) South Pole.

A penguin is hatched from 5._____ (a, an) egg. 6._____ (The, A) Emperor Penguin father hatches 7._____ (an, the) egg on 8._____ (its, their) feet and places 9._____ (a, an) flap of fatty skin over 10._____ (the, an) egg to keep 11._____ (it, them) warm.

Some penguins are very small. 12._____ (They, It) are called Blue Fairy Penguins. 13._____ (The, A) largest penguin is 14._____ (an, the) Emperor. 15._____ (It, He) can be two metres tall. 16._____ (I, She) love penguins!

5 Verbs

Present Tense Verbs

A verb is an action word.

Verbs in the present tense tell what is happening now.

Examples: runs   walks   skates

A. Look at the picture. Circle the verbs that you see in the picture.

flips   swings   skips   runs   talks   cycles

climbs   walks   throws

Regular Past Tense Verbs

A verb can tell what is happening now (present tense).
It can also tell what happened (past tense).
Most verbs have "ed" added to show past tense.
Examples: play → play**ed**   talk → talk**ed**

B. Write the past tense verbs.

1. bark _____

2. open _____

3. walk _____

4. climb _____

5. push _____

6. cook _____

C. Look at the pictures. Write the past tense verbs that show what happened.

fished   jumped   played   crawled
touched   coloured   sailed   smiled

1. _____

2. _____

3. _____

4. _____

5. _____

6. _____

7. _____

8. _____

Irregular Verbs

 Some verbs use a different word to show the past tense.
Some of the letters in the present tense verb may be in the past tense verb.
Examples: sleep → slept   dream → dreamt   fight → fought

D. **Find the past tense verb in the balloon on the right to match the present tense verb on the left. Write the pair of verbs in the spaces.**

Present Tense

feed   make
throw   lose   try
run   swim
tear   blow
drink

Past Tense

tore   made
swam   blew   lost
ran   threw
tried   fed
drank

Present	Past		Present	Past
1. _____	_____	2.	_____	_____
3. _____	_____	4.	_____	_____
5. _____	_____	6.	_____	_____
7. _____	_____	8.	_____	_____
9. _____	_____	10.	_____	_____

Some verbs have a different form for the past tense.

E. Read each sentence. Write the verb in the correct tense.

1. The children _____ (went, go) to see the circus yesterday.

2. She _____ (see, saw) them walk to the bus stop last week.

3. Where _____ (do, did) they go on their last vacation?

4. I _____ (bought, buy) a new coat last Saturday.

5. She _____ (took, takes) her brother to school every morning.

6. Mom _____ (hold, held) the baby in her arms.

7. John _____ (left, leave) for the East coast on Monday.

8. They _____ (stand, stood) outside the theatre and waited.

9. The police _____ (caught, catch) the robbers outside the bank yesterday.

10. Derek usually _____ (drinks, drank) two glasses of milk in the morning.

6 "Being" Verbs

Am, Is, Are

The "being" verbs "am", "is", and "are" tell that something is happening now.

"Am" is used with "I".

Example: I **am** a girl.

"Is" tells about one noun or pronoun.

Examples: It **is** December.   Ottawa **is** the capital of Canada.

"Are" is used with plural nouns, plural pronouns, and the word "you".

Examples: Bears **are** big.   They **are** happy.   You **are** 7 years old.

A. Read what Janet is saying. Fill in the correct "being" verbs.

1. I _____ going to Ottawa soon.

2. You _____ invited to come too.

3. It _____ a 5-hour car trip.

4. We _____ leaving at noon.

5. The capital of Canada _____ Ottawa.

6. There _____ several Parliament Buildings on the hill.

7. We _____ planning to visit them.

8. When you _____ there, you should look at all the flags.

9. There _____ 13 of them in all.

10. We _____ so excited about our trip!

Was, Were

> The "being" verbs "was" and "were" tell about something that happened in the past.
> Use "was" with one person, place, or thing.
> Use "were" with more than one person, place, or thing, or with "you".

B.   Read the sentences. Fill in the correct "being" verbs.

1. Last summer, we _____ in Alberta on holiday.

2. I _____ with my mom, my dad, and my two brothers.

3. Our visit to the Dinosaur Museum _____ very interesting.

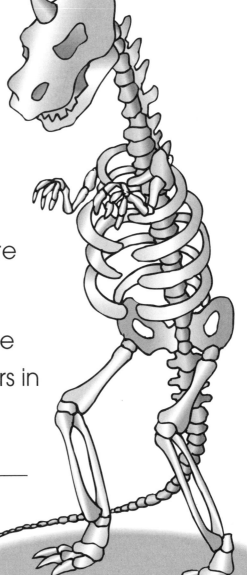

4. The dinosaur bones that _____ found in Alberta are part of the exhibit.

5. Many many years ago, there _____ many giant dinosaurs in Western Canada.

6. At that time, Canada _____ not like it is today.

7. There _____ land, sea, and flying dinosaurs.

Has, Have, Had

The "being" verbs "has" and "have" are in the present.

The being verb "had" means that it is in the past (most of the time).

Use "has" with one person, place, or thing.

Use "have" with more than one person, place, or thing.

Use "had" with both singular and plural nouns and pronouns.

C. Complete the sentences using "has", "have", or "had".

1. Colin _____ a new dog.

2. The dog _____ black markings on his hair.

3. He _____ another dog a long time ago.

4. That dog _____ a name, Blondy.

5. She _____ longer hair and was blond in colour.

6. The new dog _____ a name, Irish.

7. Colin _____ built a big dog house for Irish.

8. He and Irish _____ a lot of fun together.

9. He _____ a long leash so he can go for walks with Irish.

10. One day, when he _____ Irish on the leash, the dog ran and pulled him to the ground.

11. When Colin got up, he _____ torn his jeans.

12. He _____ also dirtied his T-shirt.

13. Colin knew that he _____ to train Irish.

"Being" Verb Review

> The present tense "being" verbs are "is", "am", "are", "has", and "have".
> The past tense "being" verbs are "was", "were", and "had".

D.   Read the story. Fill in the blanks with correct verbs.

Last week, my dad and I 1._____ (was, were) planning to go to the movies. I 2._____ (was, were) trying to decide which movie we would see. I 3._____ (has, had) three choices: *Shrek, Monsters, Inc.,* or *Atlantis.* My dad said I 4._____ (was, were) taking too long and that we 5._____ (was, were) going to be late for the movie. In the end, I 6._____ (have, had) decided I wanted to see *Shrek.*

I 7._____ (am, are) really glad we saw *Shrek.* It 8._____ (is, were) the best movie I 9._____ (has, have) seen!

7 Sentence Types

Statements

A telling sentence (statement) tells you about something.
It ends with a period (.).

Example: Beth is my friend.

A. **Look at the picture. Write telling sentences about what you see in the picture.**

1. _____

2. _____

3. _____

4. _____

5. _____

6. _____

7. _____

Questions

An asking sentence (question) asks about something.
It ends with a question mark (?).

Example: Are you having fun**?**

B.   Read the sentences below. Turn the words around to make them questions. Write the asking sentences.

The Planets

1. There are 9 planets.

    How _____

2. We live on the planet Earth.

    Which _____

3. Pluto is the farthest from the Earth.

    Which _____

4. The Earth travels around the Sun.

    Where _____

5. Saturn has 9 rings.

    How _____

6. The Sun is actually a star.

    What _____

7. My favourite planet is Jupiter.

    What _____

Commands

A command is a sentence that tells someone to do something.
It can end with a period (.) or an exclamation mark (!).

Example: Don't do that!

C. Finish the commands.

1. Don't _____

2. Take _____

3. Stop _____

4. Go _____

5. Give _____

6. Open _____

7. Show _____

D. Read each sentence. Write "C" if it is a command. Write "NC" if it is not.

1. Do the dishes!   _____

2. Take me to your leader.   _____

3. Where are you?   _____

4. Get the mower.   _____

5. Give me that!   _____

6. Do you like him?   _____

7. Don't shout here.   _____

8. It's nice.   _____

Exclamations

An exclamatory sentence (exclamation) shows strong feelings.
It ends with an exclamation mark (!).

Examples: Ouch**!**   Wow, that's great**!**

E. **Read each sentence below. Write "E" if it is an exclamatory sentence. Write "NE" if it is not.**

1. That's an amazing sunset! _____
2. It's a lovely day. _____
3. Wow, I love your dress! _____
4. Oh, no! _____
5. I hope so. _____
6. Nice to meet you. _____
7. How wonderful! _____

F. **Write 5 exclamatory sentences. Use the words in the word bank to help you.**

Wow   Oh no   Ouch   Eeek

1. _____
2. _____
3. _____
4. _____
5. _____

Nouns - Proper, Common, Plurals

A. Underline the proper nouns. Put the common nouns in parentheses ( ).

A Trip to Toronto

Our family took a trip to Toronto last July. We flew to Pearson International Airport and from there, we took a cab to our downtown hotel. The name of our hotel was the Royal York. It was very nice and very close to so many attractions.

On our first day, we went to the Hockey Hall of Fame and saw all of our favourite hockey players' memorabilia. We also went to the SkyDome for a tour. On our second day, we went up to the observation deck of the CN Tower and we had dinner at a fun restaurant called "The Old Spaghetti Factory".

What a great trip we had!

> Add "es" if the noun ends in "s", "ch", or "sh".

B. Write the plural nouns in the blanks.

1. egg _____
2. boy _____
3. dress _____
4. coat _____
5. heart _____
6. year _____
7. flower _____
8. peach _____
9. fence _____
10. brush _____

Nouns that end in "s", "x", "ch", or "sh" need an "es" to make them plural.

C. **Circle the plural nouns for words in the word bank in the word search below.**

bench
branch
bush
bus
glass
kiss
match
box
peach
fox

b	d	f	h	j	n	l	b	o	q	g
r	a	n	t	o	p	q	u	k	r	l
b	e	n	c	h	e	s	s	i	g	a
u	s	v	t	b	a	u	h	s	p	s
s	k	m	a	t	c	h	e	s	o	s
e	w	c	m	d	h	v	s	e	h	e
s	y	b	o	x	e	s	f	s	j	s
z	f	o	x	e	s	e	u	w	s	f
b	r	a	n	c	h	e	s	i	l	x

D. **Read the sentences below. Underline the singular (one) nouns and put the plural (more than one) nouns in parentheses ( ).**

1. Mom baked muffins for breakfast.

2. Alice has five brothers and a sister.

3. Andrew got new skis for his birthday.

4. Petra put the puzzles in the rack on the table.

5. The two houses are near the road.

6. There are lots of apples in that tree.

Progress Test 1

Pronouns

Some pronouns are: "I", "you", "he", "she", "it", "we", and "they".

E.   Read each sentence. Write a pronoun in place of the noun.

1.   Jim took the kite out of the box.

   _____ took _____ out of the box.

2.   The soup tastes so good.

   _____ tastes so good.

3.   Muriel rode her bike to the store.

   _____ rode _____ to the store.

4.   Franz will take some flowers to his mom.

   _____ will take some flowers to _____ .

Articles

An article helps a noun. Do you remember the use of "a", "an", and "the"?

F.   Fill in the blanks with correct articles.

1.   Did you take _____ bus downtown?

2.   I have _____ new dress; it's in _____ box.

3.   We have _____ best teacher in _____ world.

4.   Jean bought _____ ski jacket at _____ mall.

5.   _____ dog has _____ wet nose.

Verbs

Many past tense verbs have "ed" added to their present tense form.

G. Read the story. Fill in the correct verbs.

Janelle 1._____ (race, raced) home from school yesterday. She was so excited because her parents 2._____ (plan, planned) a swimming party for her birthday.

The SWIMMING PARTY

At the pool, Janelle and her friends 3._____ (float, floated) on the cool water and 4._____ (play, played) on the slide. Then, they 5._____ (kick, kicked) their feet to go faster.

I 6._____ (wish, wished) I could have a swimming party, too.

H. Change the verbs to the past tense.

1. add _____
2. pull _____
3. play _____
4. walk _____
5. open _____
6. lock _____

I. Change the past tense verbs back to the present tense.

1. crawled _____
2. sewed _____
3. pushed _____
4. barked _____
5. cooked _____
6. wanted _____

Progress Test 1

Some verbs have a different form for the past tense.

J. **Match the present tense verbs in Column A with the past tense verbs in Column B.**

Column A	Column B
1. eat	held
2. sleep	threw
3. hold	gave
4. feed	slept
5. take	ate
6. throw	fed
7. give	caught
8. catch	took

K. **Choose the correct verb in each sentence.**

1. Last summer, we _____ (go, went) to the beach.

2. I like to _____ (buy, bought) ice cream.

3. Thomas _____ (drink, drank) the milkshake.

4. The boys _____ (fight, fought) with each other yesterday.

5. She _____ (buy, bought) a new hat for her mom.

6. Rob _____ (leaves, left) for Holland this evening.

"Being" Verbs

The present tense "being" verbs are : "am", "is", "are", "has", and "have".

L. **Read the nouns or pronouns. Fill in the "being" verbs "am", "is", or "are".**

1. you _____
2. I _____
3. the dogs _____
4. we _____
5. he _____
6. cookies _____
7. they _____
8. tables _____
9. the tree _____

"Has" and "have" tell what is happening now.
"Has" is used with one person, place, or thing.
"Have" is used with "I", "you", or plural nouns and pronouns.

M. **Fill in the correct "being" verb "has" or "have".**

1. She _____ a new coat.
2. They _____ several sticks.
3. The tree _____ lots of fruit.
4. I _____ a computer.
5. You _____ my heart.

The past tense "being" verbs are "was" and "were". "Was" is used for singular noun and "were" for plurals.

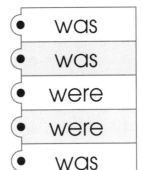

N. **Match the nouns in Column A with the verbs in Column B.**

Column A	Column B
1. The television	was
2. Boys	was
3. A cup	were
4. A zebra	were
5. Balloons	was

8 Punctuation and Capitalization

Punctuation

Every sentence ends with a punctuation mark.
A telling sentence ends with a period (.).
An asking sentence ends with a question mark (?).
An exclamatory sentence ends with an exclamation mark (!).

A. Use the correct punctuation mark to end each sentence.

1. Ouch, I hurt my finger ____

2. Did you go to see the movie ____

3. The rocking horse is broken ____

4. My name is Cathy ____

5. Where did the girls play hockey ____

6. Don't touch ____

7. When did you arrive ____

8. There are several cars in the lot ____

9. What flavour do you like best ____

10. Eeek, I saw a mouse ____

11. Don't do that ____

12. The purple sweater is my favourite ____

Contractions

A contraction is a short way of writing two words.
One or more letters are taken out and replaced with an apostrophe (').

Examples: did not → **didn't**   do not → **don't**   is not → **isn't**
are not → **aren't**

B.   Match the words in Column A with the contractions in Column B.

Column A

1   is not
2   were not
3   has not
4   do not
5   did not
6   have not
7   cannot
8   could not
9   would not
10 was not
11 should not

Column B

weren't
couldn't
wasn't
haven't
can't
shouldn't
didn't
wouldn't
don't
hasn't
isn't

Capitalization

The first word and all important words in a book title begin with capital letters.

Examples: **G**oodnight, **M**oon   **T**he **V**elveteen **R**abbit

C. **The following are all book titles. Write them again using capital letters where they belong.**

1. the three little pigs

    _____

2. frog and toad are friends

    _____

3. curious george and the man with the yellow hat

    _____

4. the princess and the pea

    _____

5. i have to go

    _____

6. love you forever

    _____

D. **Think of two of your favourite books. Write their titles on the lines below.**

1. _____

2. _____

The words in a movie title all begin with capital letters.
The words in a magazine title all begin with capital letters.

E. **Read the titles in the title box. Circle them in the word search. Write them in capital letters in the spaces.**

Title Box

atlantis   shrek   owl   chickadee
the borrowers   monsters, inc.

c	b	f	j	m	u	s	d	h	y	k	z	x
m	t	s	o	r	m	d	r	e	s	g	c	h
j	t	h	e	b	o	r	r	o	w	e	r	s
l	i	r	u	n	n	p	q	a	d	i	l	k
b	o	e	b	h	s	c	s	m	u	v	o	b
g	q	k	w	a	t	l	a	n	t	i	s	f
v	d	t	l	y	e	g	x	s	v	o	c	r
s	o	a	b	f	r	u	h	b	i	a	q	v
c	w	n	g	v	s	j	h	z	p	y	w	d
v	l	r	c	h	i	c	k	a	d	e	e	z
i	s	w	n	l	n	r	l	g	t	m	w	h
m	e	x	p	t	c	k	e	y	v	a	j	p

1. _____   2. _____

3. _____   4. _____

5. _____   6. _____

9 Adjectives

An adjective is a describing word. It tells how a thing looks.
Adjectives describe size, shape, and colour.

Examples: large   round   blue

A. **Read the underlined adjectives in the sentences below. For 1 to 4, circle the pictures that match the adjectives. For 5 and 6, colour the pictures.**

1. The <u>tiny</u> mouse ran into the hole.

2. There is a <u>round</u> balloon in the sky.

3. The giraffe has a <u>long</u> neck.

4. The <u>square</u> mirror is on the wall.

5. I have a <u>blue</u> coat.

6. My <u>purple</u> shoes are neat.

Some adjectives describe how many. This can be a specific number like "three" or a number that is not specific like "several".

Example: She owns **many** dolls.

B. Read each sentence. Fill in the missing word. Draw a picture that matches the sentence.

    eight one two four three

1. A chair has _____ legs.

2. There are _____ sides on a "STOP" sign.

3. The bike has _____ tires.

4. A unicorn has _____ horn.

5. A triangle has _____ sides.

Some adjectives describe how something feels, tastes, or smells.

Examples: The honey is **sticky**.
The **sour** lemon is on the table.
The skunk smells **foul**.

C. Draw a box around each adjective for something that you can touch, smell, or feel.

1. I bit into the juicy orange.

2. The sticky apple is covered with caramel.

3. The banana was sweet to the taste.

4. The boy is drinking hot chocolate.

5. Did you smell the rotten meat?

6. The soup is creamy.

7. The bunny is so soft.

8. It likes hard carrots.

D. Fill in the blanks with adjectives for describing things that you can touch, feel, and smell.

1. _____   2. _____

3. _____   4. _____

5. _____   6. _____

7. _____   8. _____

9. _____   10. _____

11. _____   12. _____

Comparative and Superlative Adjectives

Comparative adjectives compare two people, things, or places.

Superlative adjectives compare more than two people, things, or places.

Examples: The green ball is **larger** than the blue one.
The red ball is the **largest** of the three.

E.   **Read each sentence. Choose the adjective that describes the noun best.**

1.   We can't see any apples in the _____ (taller, tallest) tree.

2.   The _____ (bigger, biggest) car in the lot is the middle one.

3.   The _____ (smaller, smallest) angel was placed on top.

4.   It was the _____ (shorter, shortest) boy that spoke.

5.   The rectangle is _____ (bigger, biggest) than the square.

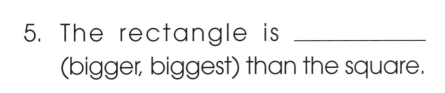

10 Parts of Sentences

Subjects

> The **subject** of a sentence tells who or what the sentence is about.
>
> *Examples*:   **John** takes the dog for a walk.
>   **The dog** ate his food.

A. Read each sentence. Underline the subject.

1. The animals were free to roam.

2. The tree grew very large.

3. The coconut was filled with milk.

4. The oranges are very juicy.

5. Candles were lit in the church.

B. Match each subject with the rest of the sentence. Draw a line to connect them.

1	The dog	•		•	scored a goal.
2	The mail carrier	•		•	taught the lesson.
3	The nurse	•		•	fed the animals.
4	The teacher	•		•	chewed the bone.
5	The hockey player	•		•	delivered the letter.
6	The zoo keeper	•		•	gave her a needle.

C. Read the sentences. Fill in the blanks with the subjects in the word bank.

> Canoes   Pioneers   Log cabins
> Vegetables   Clothes

1. _____ settled in Canada a long time ago.

2. _____ were built when land was cleared.

3. _____ like corn and carrots were grown.

4. _____ were made from the skins of animals.

5. _____ were used to travel on the water.

Riddles

D. Complete each sentence with a subject.

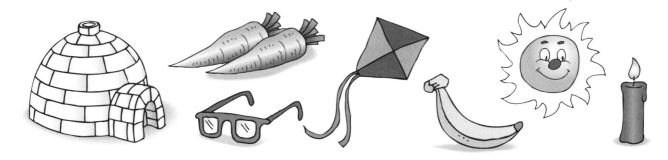

1. _____ has a yellow peel and is a sweet fruit.

2. _____ are houses made out of ice blocks.

3. _____ is a star that heats and lights the Earth.

4. _____ are what we wear to help us see better.

5. _____ are what we light on a birthday cake.

6. _____ is something that you can play with on windy days.

7. _____ are something that bunnies like.

Predicates

A predicate is the part of a sentence that tells what the subject is doing.

Examples: The car **drove down the street**.
Jim **took the dog to the vet**.

E.   Read the sentences.   Underline the predicates.

1.   The beaver is a symbol of Canada.

2.   The nickel has a beaver on its back.

3.   Beavers build dams that become their homes.

4.   Beaver dams are made of logs, sticks, and mud.

5.   The tail of a beaver is important for swimming.

F.   Complete each sentence with a predicate.

1.   The boys _____

2.   Some birds _____

3.   Giraffes _____

4.   Squares _____

5.   The zoo _____

Subject and Predicate Review

G. Read the words in the work bank. Write sentences using the words as subjects.

> triangle   mask   ball
> tree   Dad   bike   muffins
> vacation   girls   ice cream

1. _____

2. _____

3. _____

4. _____

5. _____

6. _____

7. _____

8. _____

9. _____

10. _____

> Now, read your sentences again. This time, underline the predicates you have written.

11 Subject-Verb Agreement

The subject (who or what the sentence is about) in a sentence must agree with the verb.

If the subject is singular (one), the verb must match.

Examples: The **violin is** new.
              The **boy has** a bike.

A.   Each of the following subjects is singular. Circle the verb that matches it.

1. chicken	lay	lays
2. basket	have	has
3. trip	was	were
4. book	look	looks
5. light	shines	shine
6. candle	burn	burns
7. telephone	ring	rings
8. knife	cuts	cut
9. rock	roll	rolls
10. skate	glides	glide
11. bird	fly	flies

If the subject is plural (more than one), the verb must match.

Examples: The **toys are** in the box.
The **crates fall** from the truck.

B. **Each of the following subjects is plural. Circle the verb that matches it.**

1. kangaroos — hop | hops
2. wolves — howl | howls
3. horses — gallops | gallop
4. ducks — quacks | quack
5. cats — mews | mew
6. dogs — barks | bark
7. penguins — waddles | waddle
8. monkeys — climbs | climb
9. snakes — slither | slithers
10. owls — hoot | hoots
11. whales — swims | swim
12. elephants — trumpets | trumpet
13. tigers — roar | roars

Remember! The subject of a sentence and its verb must agree. If the subject is singular, the verb must be in singular form. If the subject is plural, the verb must be in plural form. Example: The men play soccer together.

C. Read each of the following sentences. Draw a line through the verb that does not agree with the subject.

1. Magnets (is, are) objects that attract other objects.

2. They (attract, attracts) iron.

3. Paper clips (stick, sticks) to a magnet when they are close to it.

4. Magnets (has, have) two poles: north and south.

5. One pole (is, are) positive and (have, has) a "+" sign.

6. The other pole (is, are) negative and (has, have) a "–" sign.

7. The positive pole (attract, attracts) a negative pole.

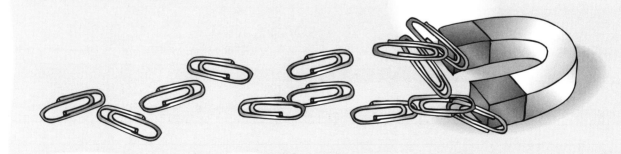

D. Complete each sentence using a verb that agrees with the subject.

live	eat	are	is	feeds	fly	flies	lays	catch

1. The bird _____ up into the nest.

2. The mother bird _____ worms to her babies.

3. When they are bigger, the baby birds _____ on their own.

4. Birds _____ in nests.

5. Penguins _____ birds that cannot fly.

6. Some birds _____ worms or fruit and some _____ fish in the sea or lakes.

7. The ostrich _____ the biggest bird in the world. It also _____ the biggest eggs.

E. Complete each sentence using a subject that agrees with the verb.

rooster	duck	owl
ostrich	chickens	

1. _____ are birds that lay eggs.

2. A _____ is a bird that quacks and swims.

3. An _____ is a bird that runs very fast.

4. A _____ is a bird that crows at sunrise.

5. An _____ is a bird that feeds at night.

12 Adverbs and Modals

Adverbs

An adverb is an action word that describes or modifies (changes) the verb in a sentence.

Adverbs often end in "ly".

Example: The cat climbed the tree.
The cat **quickly** climbed the tree.

A. Read each sentence below. Fill in the blank with an adverb that fits the sentence best from the word bank.

loudly   slowly   badly
proudly   sadly
neatly   carefully   happily

1. Justin whistled _____ as he walked home.

2. The baby banged the pots and pans _____ .

3. Maria wrote the story very _____ on the page.

4. The child crept _____ into the room where she slept.

5. Linda hurt her ankle _____ when she fell down.

6. Mike _____ showed his medal to everyone.

7. Nigel _____ placed the cover on the box.

8. With tears in her eyes, she _____ walked away.

B. Add "ly" to the words to make them adverbs.

1. careful _____
3. harsh _____
5. eager _____

2. timid _____
4. scarce _____

C. Look up the adverbs in the dictionary. Write the definitions in the spaces beside the words.

1. carefully _____

_____

2. timidly _____

_____

3. harshly _____

_____

4. scarcely _____

_____

5. eagerly _____

_____

D. Fill in the blanks with the adverbs in Exercise C.

There was 1._____ enough food for the children.
Sean 2._____ lifted the eggs out of the refrigerator
so as not to break them. He would feel bad if they broke
and he didn't want to hear his mom speak 3._____
to him. He 4._____ laid them on the counter. The
children waited 5._____ for their supper.

Modals - May and Can

Some words "help" verbs. Sometimes, they change the meanings of the sentences.

"May" is a word that gives permission.

Example: "You **may** go to the washroom," said the teacher.

"Can" is a word that means "is able to".

Example: She **can** skate faster than anyone.

E. Read the sentences below. Fill in the blanks with "can" or "may".

1. "＿＿＿＿＿＿ I go with you, Dad?" I asked.

2. They ＿＿＿＿＿＿ ride their bikes to the arena.

3. If you ＿＿＿＿＿＿ talk, then you can write.

4. You ＿＿＿＿＿＿ borrow my book.

5. ＿＿＿＿＿＿ she take me with her?

F. Write 2 sentences using "may" and 2 sentences using "can".

1. ＿＿＿＿＿＿＿＿＿＿＿＿＿＿＿＿＿＿＿＿＿＿＿＿＿＿＿＿＿＿

2. ＿＿＿＿＿＿＿＿＿＿＿＿＿＿＿＿＿＿＿＿＿＿＿＿＿＿＿＿＿＿

3. ＿＿＿＿＿＿＿＿＿＿＿＿＿＿＿＿＿＿＿＿＿＿＿＿＿＿＿＿＿＿

4. ＿＿＿＿＿＿＿＿＿＿＿＿＿＿＿＿＿＿＿＿＿＿＿＿＿＿＿＿＿＿

G. Fill in the blanks in this story with words in the word bank.

The Singer

boldly   clearly   quickly
loudly   well   quietly   hardly
proudly   happily

Whitney could sing 1._____ ; her mom 2._____ told her that she had a beautiful voice. She was 3._____ five years old when she 4._____ sang in front of everyone at school. When she finished, she 5._____ took her seat. Whitney 6._____ learned that singing 7._____ was not as important as singing 8._____ . After this discovery, she sang 9._____ all the time.

"May" means "to have permission". "Can" means "to be able to".

H. Fill in the blanks with "may" or "can".

1. When _____ you take out the garbage?

2. _____ I help you bake the cookies, Mom?

3. _____ you pass the salt to me?

4. You _____ talk in here, but you have to keep your voice low.

5. How _____ he finish his work tonight?

6. _____ the students answer your questions?

7. _____ I stay here until eight?

13 Prepositions, Antonyms, Synonyms, and Homophones

Prepositions

A preposition is a word that connects a noun or pronoun to a verb.

A. Fill in the blanks with prepositions in the word bank.

Making Honey

| of | out | with |
| in | to | upon |

Bees make honey. They fly 1._____ of the honeycomb and rest 2._____ the flowers to taste the nectar. Then they suck the nectar 3._____ of the flowers and fly back 4._____ the honeycomb 5._____ it. The queen bee lays all 6._____ the eggs. The worker bees fly 7._____ and 8._____ of the honeycomb. When all the spaces are filled 9._____ honey, a beekeeper takes it 10._____ of the honeycomb.

Prepositions of Location

Some prepositions tell where something is located.

Some of these prepositions and phrases are "under", "behind", "beside", "in front of", and "on top of".

B. Look at the pictures. Complete the sentences with the correct prepositions or phrases.

The cheese is...

1.	2.	3.	4.
_____ the table	_____ the table	_____ the table	_____ the table

C. In the boxes below, draw pictures using the prepositions or phrases given.

under	beside
in front of	on top of

Antonyms

Antonyms are words that have opposite meanings.

Examples: hot – cold   up – down

D. **Think of words that have opposite meanings to the ones below. Write them in the spaces.**

1. new _____

2. fast _____

3. quiet _____

4. in _____

5. bad _____

6. rich _____

E. **Change the meanings of these sentences by replacing the underlined words with their antonyms.**

1. The <u>big</u> _____ dog jumped over the <u>small</u> _____ cat.

2. The <u>tall</u> _____ boy is standing <u>under</u> _____ the <u>short</u> _____ bridge.

Synonyms

Synonyms are words that have the same meaning.

Examples: big – large   glad – happy

F. **Choose words that have similar meanings as the ones below. Write them in the spaces.**

| big | sad | loud | shut | under | small |

1. below _____

2. large _____

3. little _____

4. unhappy _____

5. close _____

6. noisy _____

Homophones

Words that sound alike but have different meanings are called homophones.

Examples: flower – a plant with petals
flour – a dry ingredient for baking

G.   Read the sentences below. Fill in the correct homophones.

blew   blue   see   sea   sun   son

1. The wind _____ the leaves off the tree.
2. The _____ jacket lay on the bed.
3. The _____ had many waves.
4. I _____ the beautiful flower.
5. The _____ shone brightly in the sky.
6. He took his _____ to the hockey game.

H.   Replace the underlined words with the homophones below.

A Day in the Woods

| sun | blew | week |
| deer | flower | see |

It was the last <u>weak</u> _1._____ of the holidays. Amelia picked a <u>flour</u> _2._____ from the garden. It was covered with dirt. She <u>blue</u> _3._____ the dirt off so she could <u>sea</u> _4._____ it clearly. It was a beautiful day, with the <u>son</u> _5._____ shining brightly. Even the <u>dear</u> _6._____ in the woods were happily running around.

14 Question Starters, Proofreading, and Editing

Many questions start with one of the 5 Ws – Who, What, Where, When, and Why.

A "who" question asks about a person or some persons.

A "what" question asks about some "thing".

A "where" question asks about a place.

A "when" question asks about a time.

A "why" question asks for a reason.

A. **Read each of the following statements. Write a question beginning with one of the 5 Ws that fits the statement.**

1. Who was Canada's first prime minister?

   John A. MacDonald was Canada's first prime minister.

2. _____

   They left at midnight.

3. _____

   The hat was on the rack.

4. _____

   Ray went to Alberta.

5. _____

   Kathleen was born on June 19, 1982.

6. _____

   I made a wooden horse.

Proofreading and Editing

You proofread when you re-read your writing to check for errors.
You edit when you make the corrections.

B. Check the sentences below for errors in capitalization and ending punctuation. Cross out the errors and write the corrections above them.

1. tomorrow is easter sunday?

2. she goes to vancouver every summer.

3. her birthday is february 3.

4. is mr. smith our new gym teacher.

C. Circle the incorrect punctuations. Write the correct ones in the boxes.

1. Who is your doctor. ☐

2. Don't do that? ☐

3. Take out the garbage? ☐

4. Where do you go on vacation! ☐

D. Correct the errors in this passage. Write the passage again.

The fourteenth of february is valentine's day on valentine's day, lots of people give cards and gifts to one another The heart is the symbol for this special day

There are 9 errors in this passage.

_____

_____

_____

_____

E.   Proofread the following sentences and correct the spelling errors.

1. We flw from St. John's to Halifax.   _____

2. It was a shot distance to the park.   _____

3. The flag had a maple leave on it.   _____

4. I can't weight until summer!   _____

5. The three boys raised down the street.   _____

6. Flours bloom in spring.   _____

7. I did't go to Quebec with my mom.   _____

F.   Read the passage. The incorrect spellings are underlined. Fill in the blanks with correctly-spelt words.

The Arctic is at the <u>Nouth</u> <u>Poll</u> 1._____ _____ . It is

<u>vary</u> 2._____ cold there. It is <u>colled</u> 3._____ the Tundra

because there are very few trees <u>their</u> 4._____ and a <u>not</u>

5._____ of it is covered with <u>ise</u> 6._____ and snow.

Polar bears live in the Arctic. When there is not a lot of

food <u>fro</u> 7._____ them, the polar bears will travel to <u>othr</u>

8._____ places, like Winnipeg, in search for food.

G. Read the story. Look for errors in capitalization, spelling, and punctuation. Make the corrections in the passage.

The Antarctic

Anothr name for the antarctic is the south pole. It is almost fully covred with ice and snow. Most of the ice has been on the grond for hundreds of years

penguins live on and around the Antarctic. the emperor and king penguins live closet to the south pole itself. Other penguins live near australia and Argentina.

the largest penguin is the Emperor and the smallest is the blue Fairy?

Contractions

Contractions are shorter ways of writing two or more words.

A.   Read the sentences below. Write the correct contractions in the blanks.

1.   _____ (Do not) take my toothpaste!

2.   She _____ (is not) planning to go there.

3.   They _____ (were not) able to visit their parents.

4.   Camille _____ (has not) had a good day.

5.   The children _____ (could not) ride their toboggans.

6.   His dog _____ (does not) eat meat.

7.   It seems he _____ (cannot) find the time.

8.   She _____ (will not) sing in the show.

9.   We _____ (should not) dirty the place.

10. _____ (Have not) you done your work yet?

11. _____ (Are not) you coming with us?

12. You _____ (must not) cross the road here.

Adjectives

An adjective is a word that describes or modifies (changes) a noun. It can tell something about how the noun looks, feels, tastes, or smells, and its quantity or amount.

B. Underline the adjectives in these sentences.

1. The polar bear has a white coat.

2. The penguin has oily feathers to keep it dry.

3. The snowy owl lives in the far north.

4. The giraffe has a long neck so that it can eat leaves on a tall tree.

5. The rabbit has brown fur in summer to protect it.

6. There are several species of birds.

7. The two deer ran into the woods.

8. We ate the delicious fish that we caught.

9. Many animals give birth in the Spring.

10. Some birds' eggs have a foul odour.

11. Snakes have tough skin to let them move easily.

12. There are many antelope in Africa.

Subjects and Predicates

> The subject of a sentence tells who or what the sentence is about.
> The predicate tells what the subject is doing.

C. **Read each sentence. Underline the subject and put the predicate in parentheses ( ).**

1. The holidays were happy with lots of fun.

2. People were driving home for the week.

3. Children played in the snow.

4. Shoppers bundled their packages into cars.

5. Stores stayed open late.

6. Houses shone with lights.

7. The season is a time of joy.

8. Trees are decorated carefully.

9. Cookies and cakes are baked and ready to eat.

10. People think about others.

11. They wrap their gifts.

12. Mothers, fathers, and children spend time together.

13. There is peace for a little while everywhere.

Subject-Verb Agreement

Subjects (who or what the sentences are about) and verbs must agree. If the subject is singular, the verb must be in singular form. If the subject is plural, the verb must be in plural form.

D. Read each sentence. Change the verb so that it agrees with the subject.

1. Most plants has stems, roots, leaves, and flowers. _____

2. The roots takes in water and nutrients from the soil. _____

3. The stem carry the nutrients to the leaves. _____

4. The leaves makes food. _____

5. The flower attract insects to it. _____

E. Read each sentence. Change the subject so that it agrees with the verb.

1. The <u>people</u> _____ who matters most is the child.

2. A <u>children</u> _____ needs to know that he or she is special.

3. A <u>mothers</u> _____ loves her children more than anyone.

4. Every <u>ones</u> _____ should have a happy childhood.

5. The <u>girls</u> _____ is very special and unique.

Adverbs and Modals

An adverb is a word that describes or modifies (changes) the verb in a sentence. Adverbs often end in "ly". "Can" means "is able to". "May" means "is permitted to".

F.   Fill in the blanks with the correct words.

1.   "You _____ (can, may) go with her," said Mom.

2.   The cat _____ (quickly, slowly) ran after the mouse.

3.   The little match girl _____ (sadly, happily) stood alone.

4.   Tortoises move very _____ (quickly, slowly).

5.   Ronnie _____ (can, may) race his brother.

6.   The boy _____ (proudly, quietly) showed the award he had won.

7.   The car engine roared _____ (loudly, quietly).

8.   The old woman walked _____ (timidly, loudly) down the stairs.

9.   They performed _____ (badly, hardly) at the swim meet.

10.   The winter blizzard blew _____ (scarcely, harshly) all around.

11.   There was _____ (hardly, truly) anyone there.

Prepositions, Antonyms, Synonyms, and Homophones

A preposition is a word that connects a noun and a verb. Antonyms are words with opposite meanings. Synonyms are words with similar meanings. Homophones are words that sound the same but have different meanings.

G. Circle all the prepositions in the word search.

on	onto	upon	to	out	over	of
	behind	under	with	in	beside	

k	m	d	w	x	l	j	u	p	o	n	z	c	a	k
n	h	b	e	h	i	n	d	c	y	w	d	m	s	u
n	u	y	o	u	t	b	d	o	p	w	i	t	h	m
z	c	s	c	o	v	e	r	n	g	m	p	j	r	b
t	j	k	o	b	j	f	z	t	n	u	n	d	e	r
x	l	q	n	f	l	q	t	o	f	k	t	l	s	q
b	e	s	i	d	e	n	b	w	d	p	o	c	i	n

H.   Read the pairs of words. Write "A" if they are antonyms, "S" if they are synonyms, and "H" if they are homophones.

1. under – over _____
2. up – down _____
3. blew – blue _____
4. small – large _____
5. huge – enormous _____
6. unhappy – sad _____
7. noisy – quiet _____
8. tall – short _____
9. bad – good _____
10. hot – cold _____
11. new – old _____
12. sun – son _____
13. glad – happy _____
14. flour – flower _____
15. angry – mad _____
16. dear – deer _____

Vocabulary & Usage

Creatures of the Galapagos Islands

1

The Galapagos Islands are located approximately 950 kilometres off the coast of South America. These islands are famous for their <u>unique</u> vegetation and wildlife. Two of the unusual <u>creatures</u> found on these islands are the Galapagos Tortoise and the Marine Iguana.

The Galapagos Tortoise is the largest living tortoise. It has a huge shell made of bone. A male tortoise can grow to be over one metre long and can have a mass of over 200 kilograms. It can <u>effortlessly</u> carry a full-grown adult on its back. This slow-moving reptile has elephant-like feet with short toes. The Galapagos Tortoise is a <u>herbivore</u> that eats prickly pear cactus and fruits, water ferns, leaves, and grasses. During the day, this animal can <u>typically</u> be found <u>basking</u> in the hot sun or cooling itself in a lake or under a shady tree. A Galapagos Tortoise has another amazing <u>characteristic</u>. It can live to be 100 to 150 years old.

Another <u>extraordinary</u> animal found on the rocky shoreline of the Galapagos Islands is the Marine Iguana. This reptile is the only sea-going lizard in the world. It has razor-sharp teeth and long claws. It can grow to <u>approximately</u> one metre in length. The Marine Iguana feeds on marine algae and seaweed found on either <u>exposed</u> rocks or in the cold seawater. The Marine Iguana spends much of its day lying in the sun warming its body and then diving into the ocean to find something to eat.

A. Use the underlined words in the passage to complete the crossword puzzle.

Across

A. not exactly

B. uncovered, without protection

C. lying in warmth and sunshine

D. an animal that feeds mainly on plants

E. any living persons or animals

Down

1. having no like or equal

2. feature that makes something recognizable

3. involving little or no effort

4. representing a particular type of person or thing

5. different from others

B. Using the information found in the passage, complete the following Venn Diagram.

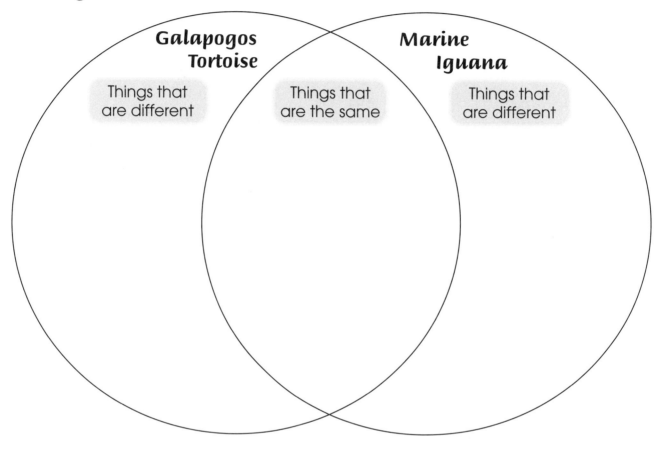

C. Using the information from the Venn Diagram, write two paragraphs to show how the Galapagos Tortoise and the Marine Iguana are alike and different. Title your work. The first sentence is done for you.

_____

The Galapagos Tortoise and the Marine Iguana are alike and different in many ways.

First they are alike because _____

_____

_____

_____

_____

They are different because _____

_____

_____

_____

D. **Read the words in each row. Cross out the word which <u>does not</u> belong and, on the line below, give the reason. Write a new word that <u>does</u> belong in the list.**

1. turtle   iguana   fish   monkey

    Reason _____

    New Word _____

2. Cuba   Jamaica   Galapagos   Canada

    Reason _____

    New Word _____

3. ocean   park   river   pond

    Reason _____

    New Word _____

4. shoe   crown   wig   helmet

    Reason _____

    New Word _____

2 Bet You Can't Eat Just One

Popcorn, peanuts, and tortilla chips are just some examples of well-liked snack foods. However, the most popular of all snacks are potato chips. People who enjoy this <u>crispy</u> treat would agree that it just takes one chip to tease the taste buds on the tongue creating a craving for more. This <u>tasty</u> treat was accidentally invented in 1853 in Saratoga Springs, New York.

George Crum was a chef in a restaurant where french fries were a popular menu item. One day a diner complained that the fries were too thick and soggy so he sent his plate back to the kitchen. George Crum, hoping to <u>satisfy</u> the customer, made a thinner <u>batch</u> of french fries. The man was still unhappy. Crum felt insulted and was <u>angry</u> with the customer. He decided to annoy this <u>fussy</u> man. He made paper-thin fries which he cooked in boiling oil. He salted these crispy potato slices and then served them to the man. The customer, <u>surprisingly</u> enough, loved them and potato chips were invented.

News of this creation spread and soon other people began making their own versions of this delicious treat. People everywhere developed a love for potato chips. In 1895, the first potato chip factory was opened and potato chips became available in grocery stores. Today most people would agree that when it comes to eating potato chips, it is <u>difficult</u> to have just one.

A. Find the underlined words in the story. Match each word in Column A with its synonym in Column B.

Column A

1. ( ) crispy
2. ( ) tasty
3. ( ) satisfy
4. ( ) batch
5. ( ) angry
6. ( ) fussy
7. ( ) surprisingly
8. ( ) difficult

Column B

A annoyed
B hard
C crunchy
D choosy
E delicious
F please
G bunch
H amazingly

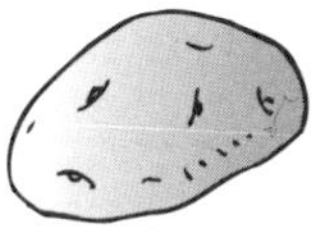

B. You are a reporter for the Saratoga Springs News and have just witnessed the invention of potato chips. Complete the chart below to record important information about this event.

Who was involved?	
What was the event?	
Where was the event taking place?	
When did this event happen?	
How did this happen?	

C. Using the information from the chart, write a news story about this event.

_____
(Newspaper Name)

_____
(Date)

_____
(Article Title)

_____
(Reporter's Name)

_____

_____

_____

_____

_____

_____
(Caption)

_____

_____

_____

_____

_____

_____

_____

D. Look at the following words. Underline the base word. Use the word in a sentence to show its meaning. The first one is done for you.

A **prefix** is attached to the beginning of a base word. It can be used to help find the meanings of new words. The prefix "un" means "not".

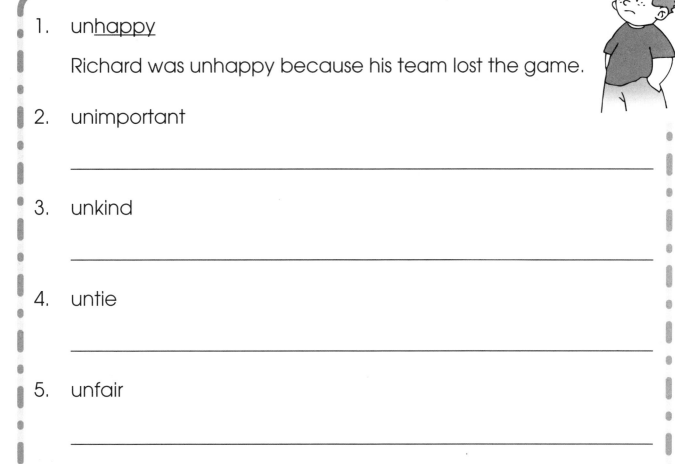

1. un<u>happy</u>

   Richard was unhappy because his team lost the game.

2. unimportant

   _____

3. unkind

   _____

4. untie

   _____

5. unfair

   _____

6. unpopular

   _____

7. unsafe

   _____

8. untrue

   _____

3 Barbie Hits the Track

At first glance, Ashley Taws seems to be an ordinary young lady. She loves basketball, softball, volleyball, and snowboarding. She has three dogs and a cat, and a fear of ladybugs. The one thing that does set her apart from other girls her age is that she is a race car driver.

Ashley was born on November 1, 1983 in Toronto, Ontario. She began racing Go Karts at the age of nine but quickly progressed to racing faster karts. Ashley won in many races. At the age of sixteen, Ashley moved from racing Go Karts to car racing. In 2001, she caught the attention of her fans by driving a flashy looking pink and purple car. With her "*Be anything with Barbie at WAL-MART*" car, she finished her year in second place in the overall standings and received a trophy for her sportsmanship. It seemed as if Ashley were on her way to a promising racing career.

Unfortunately, on December 7, 2002 Ashley was seriously hurt in a car accident. She broke her back, had internal injuries, and also damaged her leg. At first, Ashley worried that she would never be able to race again, but with determination she worked hard to regain her strength and movement. Seven months after her accident, Ashley competed in her first race in Toronto. She finished in fourth place. It was a great day for Ashley and for her many supportive fans.

A. Complete the crossword puzzle with words from the reading passage.

Across
A. advanced
B. normal or usual
C. get back
D. severely

Down
1. likely to succeed
2. inside of something
3. job or occupation
4. showy and stylish
5. prize

3

B. Ashley Taws is coming to speak to your class about her experiences as a race car driver. Write five questions that you would like to ask her.

1. _____

2. _____

3. _____

4. _____

5. _____

C. To convince people, it is important to understand both sides of an opinion. Read the statement below and complete the chart.

I should be allowed to race Go Karts.

Reasons For	Reasons Against
1. Racing is very exciting.	1. Racing is dangerous.
2. _____	2. _____
3. _____	3. _____
4. _____	4. _____

D. Write a letter to convince your parents to let you play a sport that they do not want you to play.

Dear Mom and Dad,

I know that you do not want me to _____

_____ but I think that it is a great idea. I would like to

_____ because

_____

_____

_____

_____

_____

_____

_____

_____

_____

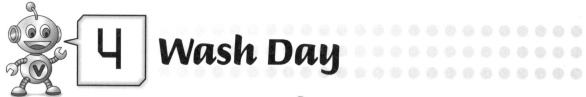

4 Wash Day

A. Read the following story. Use the words in the word bank to fill in the blanks.

towel	shiny	rinsed	lastly
allowed	first	bead	next

Michael stared as his big brother Larry backed his 1._____ black 1964 Mustang out of the garage. For years Michael had watched as Larry carefully went through the steps of washing and caring for his car. Today was finally the day that Michael was being 2._____ to help.

3._____ , Larry instructed Michael to use the hose to wet the car thoroughly from top to bottom. This helped to remove any loose dirt. 4._____ , Larry filled the bucket with cold water and added a special car soap which made the water sudsy. Michael was instructed to dunk a clean cotton 5._____ into the soapy water and gently wash the car. Together the brothers washed the roof, hood, and trunk of the car. Michael then 6._____ these areas with clean water from the hose. Next, they washed the sides and the bumpers of the car. Once again, Larry told Michael to hose off the soapsuds on the car. 7._____ , it was time to dry the car. Michael and Larry each grabbed a clean dry towel and began wiping the car surface. Again, they started with the roof, hood, and trunk and then moved to the sides of the car. After the last 8._____ of water was wiped off, both boys stepped back to admire the great work they had done.

B. Look at the group of pictures below. Put the pictures in order by writing "first", "next", or "last" under the correct picture.

C. Write a paragraph about how to do ONE of the following.

How to brush your teeth
How to build a snow fort
How to care for a pet

Use the words "first", "next", and "last" to help put steps in order.

_____

_____

_____

_____

_____

_____

Homonyms are words that sound the same but have different spellings and meanings.

D. Fill in each blank with the correct homonym.

1. Bruce _____ (knew, new) that Michelle would enjoy using the hose.

2. It took _____ (for, four) hours to wash the car.

3. After running the marathon, Rob felt _____ (week, weak).

4. Jennifer wore an old _____ (pair, pear) of sneakers to clean the garage.

5. Can you _____ (hear, here) the thunder in the distance?

E. The wrong homonyms have been used in the following sentences. Rewrite each sentence using the proper homonym.

1. The be buzzed around the flour garden.

_____

2. The wind blue leaves onto the freshly washed car.

_____

3. Michael could sea how special the car was to Larry.

_____

4. There were ate kittens at the pet store.

_____

5. Sandra walked to the store to bye milk.

_____

F. Change one letter in each slide to make the final word. Each slide must be a real word.

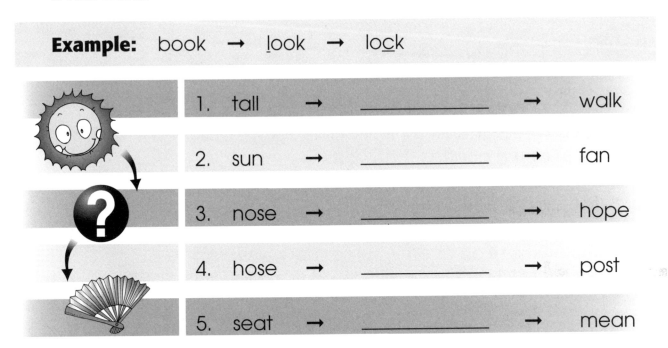

Example: book → l̲ook → loc̲k

1. tall → _____ → walk

2. sun → _____ → fan

3. nose → _____ → hope

4. hose → _____ → post

5. seat → _____ → mean

Make up your own word slides. Challenge a friend to solve them.

1. [_____] ➡ _____ ➡ [_____]

2. [_____] ➡ _____ ➡ [_____]

5 Animal Pals

Everyone needs a friend they can depend on. Friends can be great company and will lend a helping hand whenever they can. Just as human beings depend on their friends, animals depend on each other too.

The giraffe is an example of an animal which has developed a special friendship with a small bird called an oxpecker. In Africa, oxpeckers can usually be seen riding on the back or the head of a giraffe. One may think that a passenger of this type would be annoying, but the giraffe and the little bird depend on each other for meals and for protection from their enemies.

The oxpecker gets its meals by using its thick beak to eat the fleas, ticks, and flies off the skin of the giraffe. It helps its friend by munching on annoying pests that are in hard-to-reach places. With its buddy on board, the giraffe eats leaves off the trees knowing that the oxpecker will make a noise if an enemy comes near. In turn, the oxpecker is safe because it is perched comfortably on the giraffe, out of reach from its enemies.

It's easy to see how these two animals depend on their friendship for survival in the wild.

A. Fill in the blanks to make synonyms for words found in the story.

> *Synonyms* are words that have the same meaning.

1. **little**   a. s _ _ _ l   b. t _ _ y

2. **depend**   a. r _ _ y   b. n _ e _

3. **munching**   a. _ a t _ _ _   b. c _ _ w _ _ _

4. **skin**   a. f _ _   b. _ o a _

5. **friend**   a. c h _ _   b. _ _ l

B. Use information from the story to write an acrostic poem about the giraffe. Don't forget to mention the oxpecker.

5

C. Complete the crossword puzzle by finding opposites.

Collective Nouns

Collective nouns are words that name a group of things.

Examples: A **flock** of sheep

A **team** of players

D.   **Match each collective noun with the correct group.**

1. A school of ⬤   A. lions

2. A swarm of ⬤   B. fish

3. An army of ⬤   C. cows

4. A herd of ⬤   D. bees

5. A pride of ⬤   E. ants

6. A litter of ⬤   F. puppies

E.   **The oxpecker spends a lot of time riding on the giraffe. Create a comic strip about these two animals. Use talk balloons to show what they might say to each other.**

The Giraffe & The Oxpecker

6 Penelope and Her Plastic Palm Tree

Penelope Patterson appeared to be an ordinary 10-year-old girl. She lived with her mother, father, and her brother Paul on Pine Street in Peterborough, Ontario. She had a pet poodle named Poncho and purple was her favourite colour. Penelope loved to play with her two best friends, Patty and Priscilla.

Penelope had everything she ever wanted except for one thing. She dreamed of having her own plastic palm tree. Her parents refused to buy one for her birthday and Santa did not bring one at Christmas. Penelope decided to take matters into her own hands. She asked her mother to take her to the bank. Penelope withdrew enough money from her account to buy the magnificent plastic palm tree. Penelope's mother then drove to the local department store where Penelope bought the tree. As soon as they arrived home, Penelope placed her tree right in the middle of the front lawn.

Penelope loved her plastic palm tree. Her family tolerated the tree but the neighbours hated it. They felt that the tree made the neighbourhood look terrible. In fact, they disliked it so much that they sent a petition around the community. All the neighbours signed the petition that ordered Penelope to remove the tree from the front yard. Penelope was devastated. What would she do?

Suddenly Penelope had a brilliant idea. She decided to write a speech to convince her neighbours to let the tree stay in the front yard.

A. Help Penelope brainstorm ideas for her speech. Fill in the thought bubble with reasons for keeping the tree.

Think Before You Write !

_____

_____

_____

_____

_____

B. Using the information from above, help Penelope complete her speech.

Fellow Neighbours,

    I have gathered you here today for a very important reason. I would like to talk to you about _____

_____

_____

_____

_____

_____

_____

C. The following is a list of "p" words found in the story. Place them in alphabetical order.

Patty   Pine   parents   placed
Penelope   Patterson   Paul   pet
poodle   Poncho   purple   plastic
petition   Priscilla   palm   Peterborough

1. _____
2. _____
3. _____
4. _____
5. _____
6. _____
7. _____
8. _____

9. _____
10. _____
11. _____
12. _____
13. _____
14. _____
15. _____
16. _____

D. Write the contraction for each pair of words.

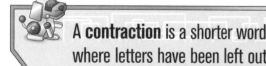 A **contraction** is a shorter word made from two words. An apostrophe (') is used to show where letters have been left out.

1. he is   _____
2. would not   _____

3. they are   _____
4. I will   _____

5. it is   _____
6. I would   _____

E. Write the words used to make the contractions.

1. couldn't _____

2. we've _____

3. I'm _____

4. she'll _____

5. that's _____

6. you're _____

F. Using contractions, rewrite what Penelope is saying.

1. I will write a speech about my plastic palm tree.

   _____

2. It would not make sense to get rid of such a beautiful tree.

   _____

Alliteration

Alliteration is a consonant sound repeated.

Examples: **P**enelope **p**layed near her **p**lastic **p**alm tree.
Six **s**wans **s**wam **s**lowly in the **s**un.

G. Write silly sentences using words beginning with the letters provided.

1. **B** _____

2. **W** _____

3. **D** _____

7 The Night the Lights Went out

It was a hot and <u>humid</u> summer evening. Kevin and his brother Alan were playing catch in the backyard. They decided to go inside to grab a drink and cool off in their air-conditioned house. Kevin opened the refrigerator and took out a <u>pitcher</u> full of lemonade. He poured a glass for himself and a glass for Alan. The boys decided to watch television. Suddenly, something <u>unusual</u> happened. The TV <u>flickered</u> and turned off. Alan tried to use the remote control to turn it back on, but nothing happened. They soon realized that the power was off. What would they do? They couldn't play video games or use the computer. That <u>required</u> electricity. They couldn't play their CDs or listen to the radio. That also required electricity.

Kevin suggested going outside to do some stargazing. Without streetlights, the stars were bright and easy to see. The boys made themselves <u>comfortable</u> in the lawn chairs. Lying on their backs, they saw the Big Dipper, Orion's Belt, and they even saw the planet Mars. It was an incredible sight. Kevin and Alan had never realized how <u>spectacular</u> the night sky could be.

After <u>gazing</u> at the stars for an hour, the boys went into the house. It was very dark except for a few candles that their parents had lit. They wondered what they would do for the <u>remainder</u> of the evening. Mom and Dad had some great ideas. The family spent the night playing cards and board games and telling ghost stories in the candlelight. Kevin and Alan had never <u>imagined</u> that being without electricity could be so much fun.

A. Match each of the following words from the passage with the proper definition.

1.	◯	humid
2.	◯	pitcher
3.	◯	unusual
4.	◯	flickered
5.	◯	required
6.	◯	comfortable
7.	◯	spectacular
8.	◯	gazing
9.	◯	remainder
10.	◯	imagined

A. impressive or dramatic to look at

B. moved with a jerky motion

C. moist or damp

D. formed an idea in the mind

E. the part of something left over

F. large jug with one handle

G. looking for a long time

H. out of the ordinary

I. needed

J. feeling comfort or at ease

B. Kevin and Alan discovered that there are many fun things to do that do not require electricity. Suggest 4 such activities.

1. _____

2. _____

3. _____

4. _____

C. Match the words in Column A with the words in Column B to make compound words. Write the new words on the lines.

Column A

1. down
2. paper
3. candle
4. out
5. every
6. him
7. news
8. fire

Column B

paper
side
place
self
back
stairs
one
light

1. _____   2. _____

3. _____   4. _____

5. _____   6. _____

7. _____   8. _____

Adjectives

An adjective is a word that describes a person, place, or thing.

Examples: The **dark** sky was filled with **bright** stars.

D. Circle the two adjectives in each sentence.

1. The friendly neighbour sat on the comfortable chair.

2. The red planet could be seen in the dark sky.

3. The tasty lemonade was made from fresh lemons.

4. The wax candle had an orange flame.

5. The playful puppy caught the rubber ball.

6. My wonderful mother cooked a delicious dinner.

7. The noisy children are running around in the small room.

8. The tired boys rested in the cool shade.

E. Add an adjective to each underlined noun. Write the new sentence.

1. The <u>firefighter</u> sprayed water on the <u>fire</u>.

_____

_____

2. The <u>airplane</u> is in the <u>sky</u>.

_____

_____

3. A <u>boat</u> took us to the <u>island</u>.

_____

_____

4. The <u>car</u> belongs to the <u>man</u>.

_____

_____

5. The <u>children</u> share the <u>cake</u>.

_____

_____

A. Read the following story. Use the words in the word bank to fill in the blanks.

original   tower   traffic
fire   electricity
invented   ancient   guide
candles   brighter

A lighthouse is a tall 1._____ with a very bright light at the top. It is usually located near the coast to 2._____ sailors at night and to warn them of points of danger. The lighthouse acts as a 3._____ sign on the sea.

Lighthouses have been around for a very long time. In fact, the 4._____ Egyptians built the first one, the Pharos of Alexandria, in 280 B.C. It was the height of a 45-storey building. An open 5._____ at the top was used as a source of light.

Later in the history of lighthouses, 6._____ were used to create light until the oil lamp was 7._____ . In the late 1700's, a bowl mirror was put behind the flame of an oil lamp and this created a beam of light. The mirror made the light 8._____ and easier to see from a distance. In 1886, the Statue of Liberty became the first lighthouse to use 9._____ .

Today there are about 1,400 lighthouses in the world. Most of them are automated but a few have been left in their 10._____ state to remind us of their important role in history.

B. Match the following words with the proper definition.

1. ◯ basking   A. job or occupation

2. ◯ approximately   B. moist or damp

3. ◯ exposed   C. not exactly

4. ◯ ordinary   D. moved with a jerky motion

5. ◯ career   E. lying in warmth and sunshine

6. ◯ humid   F. uncovered without protection

7. ◯ flickered   G. showy and stylish

8. ◯ flashy   H. normal or usual

C. Match each word in Column A with its synonym in Column B.

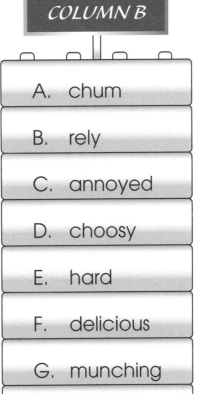

COLUMN A	COLUMN B
1. ____ angry	A. chum
2. ____ difficult	B. rely
3. ____ tasty	C. annoyed
4. ____ depend	D. choosy
5. ____ friend	E. hard
6. ____ fussy	F. delicious
7. ____ tiny	G. munching
8. ____ chewing	H. little

D. Read the words in each row. Cross out the word which does not belong and on the line below, give the reason. Write a new word that does belong in the list.

1. | dog   elephant   cat   hamster |

Reason: _____

New Word: _____

2. | sock   shoe   belt   slipper |

Reason: _____

New Word: _____

3. | soccer   swimming   baseball   golf |

Reason: _____

New Word: _____

E. Fill in each blank with the correct homonym.

1. Olivia picked a juicy _____ (pair, pear) from the tree.

2. The ship's captain _____ (heard, herd) the foghorn blow.

3. The _____ (sail, sale) on the boat was pure white.

4. The _____ (son, sun) was setting in the west.

5. It took one _____ (weak, week) to drive to Vancouver.

F. Change one letter in each slide to make the final word. Each slide should be a real word.

1. son ••••▶ _____ ••••▶ fun

2. nose ••••▶ _____ ••••▶ hope

3. same ••••▶ _____ ••••▶ camp

4. ran ••••▶ _____ ••••▶ cat

5. win ••••▶ _____ ••••▶ pan

G. Match the word in Column A with its opposite in Column B.

Column A	Column B
1. ◯ best	A. thin
2. ◯ hard	B. far
3. ◯ thick	C. worst
4. ◯ front	D. first
5. ◯ last	E. soft
6. ◯ near	F. back

H. Write the contraction for each pair of words.

1. I will _____   2. You are _____

3. that is _____   4. they are _____

5. I am _____   6. could not _____

I. **Match the words in Column A with the words in Column B to make compound words.**

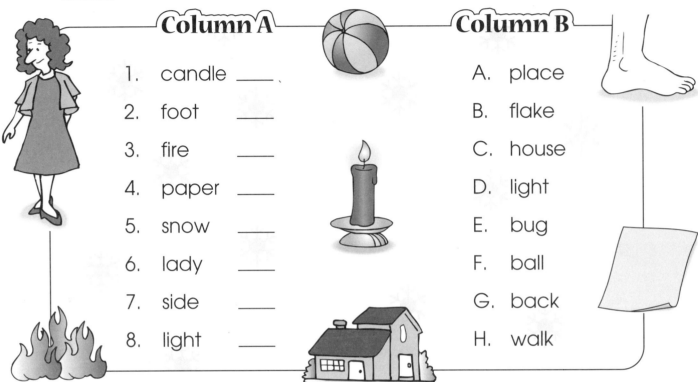

Column A

1. candle ____
2. foot ____
3. fire ____
4. paper ____
5. snow ____
6. lady ____
7. side ____
8. light ____

Column B

A. place
B. flake
C. house
D. light
E. bug
F. ball
G. back
H. walk

J. **Underline the base word in the following words. Use the word in a sentence to show its meaning.**

1. unsafe _____

_____

2. unlock _____

_____

3. untie _____

_____

4. untidy _____

_____

5. unhappy _____

_____

K. **Circle the two adjectives in each sentence.**

1. The tall ship sailed toward the bright light.

2. The wise captain was avoiding the rocky shore.

3. The playful dolphins swam in the blue ocean.

4. The tiny canoe swayed in the salty sea.

5. The old lighthouse used wax candles to make a light.

L. **Read the following paragraph. Circle the six misspelled words and write the correct words on the lines below.**

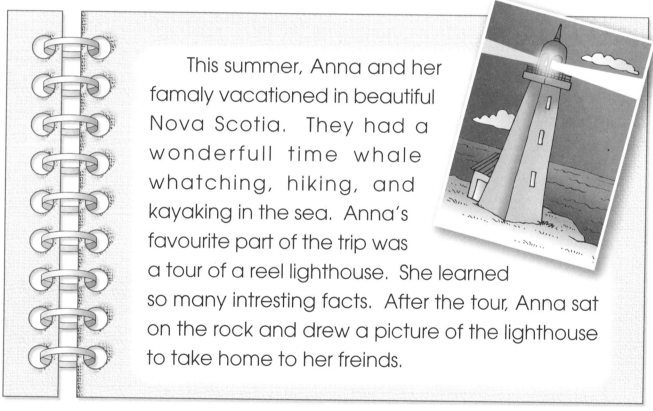

This summer, Anna and her famaly vacationed in beautiful Nova Scotia. They had a wonderfull time whale whatching, hiking, and kayaking in the sea. Anna's favourite part of the trip was a tour of a reel lighthouse. She learned so many intresting facts. After the tour, Anna sat on the rock and drew a picture of the lighthouse to take home to her freinds.

1. _____   2. _____

3. _____   4. _____

5. _____   6. _____

8 | The Three-Toed Sloth

The <u>tropical</u> rainforest is home to a large number of unusual creatures. There are insects, reptiles, <u>amphibians</u>, birds, and mammals. Most of the animals live on the forest floor. Only a few can be found living in the treetops. One of these <u>extraordinary</u> treetop creatures is the sloth.

The sloth is a slow moving mammal that spends most of its life hanging upside down in the <u>canopy</u> of the rainforest. It eats, sleeps, mates, and gives birth while upside down.

A sloth is about the size of a cat. It has a short, flat head, big eyes, a short nose, and tiny ears. It has a <u>stubby</u> tail, long legs, and curved claws which it uses to hang from trees.

Sloths have brown fur but the fur usually has greenish-coloured algae growing on it. The algae act as a <u>camouflage</u> to protect the sloth from its enemies.

The sloth is a <u>herbivore</u>, which means that it only eats plants. It munches on leaves, fruits, and twigs during the night. The sloth can live with very little food. It gets its water from eating juicy leaves and licking dew drops.

People see the sloth as a very <u>lazy</u> creature. This may be because it spends 15 to 18 hours sleeping each day and because it <u>rarely</u> leaves the canopy of the rainforest.

The sloth is <u>definitely</u> an interesting animal that lives a slow-paced life. Perhaps people should be more like the sloth and slow down. What do you think?

A. Use the underlined words in the passage to complete the crossword puzzle.

ACROSS

A. unwilling to do work
B. not very often
C. certainly or surely
D. tops of trees that form a ceiling
E. very unusual

DOWN

1. animal that eats plants
2. very hot and humid
3. short and thick
4. disguise
5. cold-blooded animals that live first in water, then on land

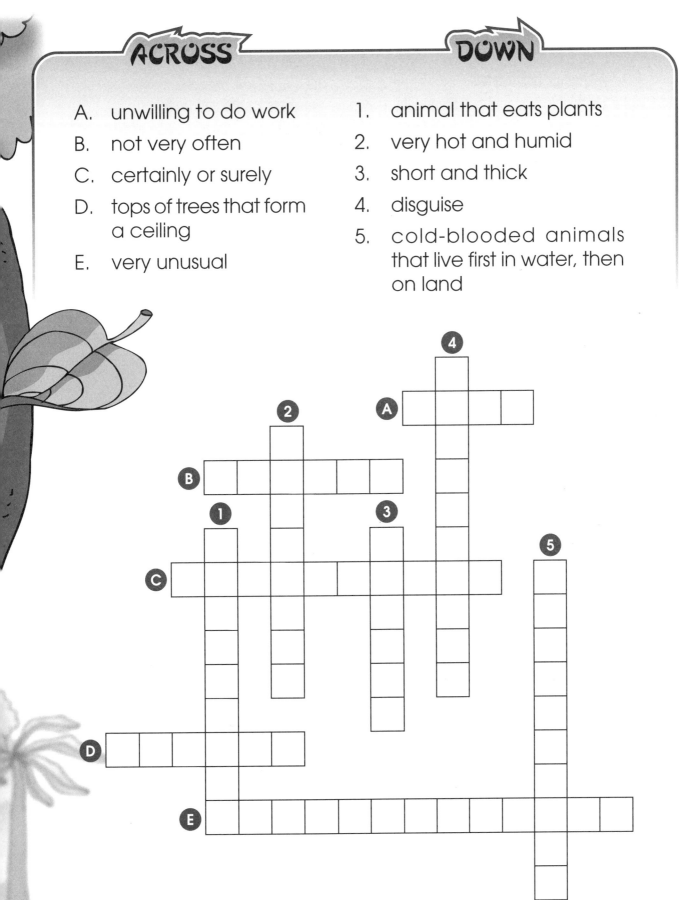

8

Limerick

A limerick is a funny poem.

- A limerick has five lines.
- Lines one, two, and five rhyme and they have the same length and rhythm.
- Lines three and four rhyme. They are shorter than the other lines.
- Most limericks begin with **There once was a...**

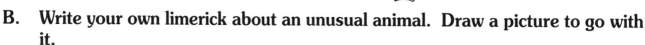

There once was a sloth named Bo
Who often had no place to go.
Along branches he'd creep,
Upside down he'd sleep.
That sloth he's so very slow.

B. Write your own limerick about an unusual animal. Draw a picture to go with it.

Line 1
_____

Line 2
_____

Line 3
_____

Line 4
_____

Line 5
_____

C. Match each of the following idioms with its meaning. Write the letters.

> *An **idiom** is an expression that has a meaning that is not the usual meaning of the words.*

1. Don't put the cart before the horse.
2. I have butterflies in my stomach.
3. I was shaking in my boots.
4. I have my hands full.
5. Hold your horses.
6. I'm in hot water.

A. Don't do things in the wrong order.
B. Be patient and wait.
C. I have a lot to do.
D. I'm in trouble.
E. I was afraid.
F. I'm nervous.

1	2	3	4	5	6

D. Read each of the idioms. Draw a picture of what you actually see when you say the phrase.

Who let the cat out of the bag?	I put my foot in my mouth.

9 The Dead Sea

Rivers, lakes, seas, and oceans are all bodies of water that cover parts of the earth. Rivers and lakes are usually surrounded by land and are made up of fresh water. Seas and oceans are much larger. They are made up of salt water. The Dead Sea is an interesting body of water because although it is a sea, it is also very similar to a lake.

Dead Sea

The countries of Jordan and Israel surround the Dead Sea. The Jordan River flows into the Dead Sea, but there is no place for the water to flow out. The only way for the water to escape from the Dead Sea is through evaporation. Evaporation happens when water is heated by the sun and changes from liquid to vapour. As vapour, water is carried into the air and becomes part of the clouds. As the water evaporates, salt is left behind. As a result, the Dead Sea is very, very salty. In fact, it is the saltiest body of water in the world. Fish and plants cannot survive in this deadly environment, but human beings can safely take pleasure in its unique characteristics.

Thousands of people visit the Dead Sea each year to enjoy its mineral-rich waters. The large amounts of salt make it difficult to swim in the sea so people just sit back and float like a boat on water. The water does the work while the tourists take in the beautiful scenery.

A. Match each of the following words from the passage with the proper definition.

1. ____ surrounded
2. ____ escape
3. ____ evaporation
4. ____ liquid
5. ____ environment
6. ____ survive
7. ____ characteristics
8. ____ scenery

A. natural world where people, animals, and plants live

B. manage to stay alive

C. come all around completely

D. features that make somebody or something recognizable

E. natural surroundings

F. get free

G. fluid, not solid

H. a process in which water is changed from liquid to vapour

B. Read the following words. Write the number of syllables.

Number of Syllables

1. escape   2
2. environment   ____
3. rivers   ____
4. similar   ____
5. surrounded   ____
6. thousands   ____
7. survive   ____
8. mineral   ____

9

Challenge

Find a word in the story that has five syllables.

_____

C. Write the plural form of these words.

Most words are made plural by adding "s".

If a word ends in "y", we change the "y" to "i" and add "es".

For words ending in "s", "ss", "ch", "sh", "x", and "z", add "es" to make plurals.

1. sea _____   2. box _____

3. body _____   4. country _____

5. address _____ 6. lunch _____

7. river _____   8. wish _____

9. ocean _____   10. buzz _____

D. Write the singular form of these words.

1. lakes _____   2. guesses _____

3. berries _____ 4. peaches _____

5. ladies _____   6. foxes _____

7. tourists _____ 8. bushes _____

E. Read the question in each box. Write the answer with describing words.

> *Think about a day when you were at the beach or at a swimming pool. Maybe you were floating in the water or playing in the sand.*

Sights

How did the people and things around you look?

_____

_____

_____

_____

_____

Sounds

How did the water and things around you sound?

_____

_____

_____

_____

_____

Touch

How did the water or sand feel?

_____

_____

_____

_____

Feelings

How did you feel on this day?

_____

_____

_____

_____

10 The Story of Chocolate

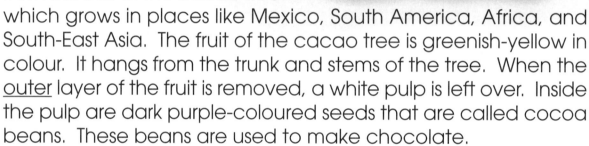

Chocolate

is a favourite "sweet treat" of people all over the world. It comes from the fruit of the cacao tree which grows in places like Mexico, South America, Africa, and South-East Asia. The fruit of the cacao tree is greenish-yellow in colour. It hangs from the trunk and stems of the tree. When the <u>outer</u> layer of the fruit is removed, a white pulp is left over. Inside the pulp are dark purple-coloured seeds that are called cocoa beans. These beans are used to make chocolate.

The native people discovered the cacao tree early in their history. They would use the beans to <u>make</u> a <u>delicious</u> drink which we now know as "hot chocolate". The beans were so <u>valuable</u> to some native groups that they would use them as money.

During the age of exploration, chocolate was introduced to the rest of the world. In 1502, Columbus noticed the natives trading in beans for other goods, but he did not understand their worth. In 1519, another Spanish <u>explorer</u> by the name of Cortez learned the <u>secret</u> of the cocoa bean from the Aztecs of Mexico. It became an <u>instant</u> hit when the Queen had her first <u>sip</u> of hot chocolate flavoured with chili peppers.

At first, only the very <u>rich</u> could afford to have chocolate, but soon the French, English, and Dutch began to grow cacao trees in their colonies. In no time at all, people were enjoying chocolate all over Europe. Later, the chili pepper was replaced with sugar. Chocolate began to be used to make chocolate bars and a wide <u>variety</u> of desserts. The rest, as they say, is history!

A. Read each sentence. Choose a word from the story that means the same as the underlined word.

1. What <u>type</u> of plants will you put in the garden?

2. Let's <u>create</u> a snowman.

3. The <u>external</u> part of an orange is called the peel.

4. The <u>wealthy</u> man drove an expensive car.

5. The diamond ring was extremely <u>precious</u> to her.

6. The song was an <u>immediate</u> hit on the radio.

7. The children discovered the <u>mystery</u> of the map.

8. The <u>traveller</u> saw many parts of the world.

9. Mom baked a <u>tasty</u> apple pie.

10. I had a small <u>drink</u> of Dad's tea.

B. Make a list of eight chocolate bars. Arrange them in ABC order.

Remember to use a capital letter to name each chocolate.

Chocolate Bars

1.
2.
3.
4.
5.
6.
7.
8.

C. Brainstorm three things to fit in each category below. An example is given.

1. **Things Made with Chocolate**

    Black forest cake

2. **Special Days When Chocolate is Shared**

    Halloween

3. **Things That Taste Great with Chocolate**

    Almonds

Challenge

cool   late

How many words can you make using the letters in the word "chocolate"? Two examples are given.

D. You have invented a new chocolate bar. In the space below, design a poster to advertise your new creation.

Be sure to give your chocolate bar a catchy name.

11 Dr. Know-It-All

Dr. Know-It-All is the advice doctor for Fairy Tale Characters. Below is an example of letters he receives and the advice that he gives.

Dear Dr. Know-It-All,

Today my mother asked me to sell the cow at the market because our family needs the money. When I took it to be sold, a man offered me some magic beans for the cow. He told me that the beans would bring riches for my family. When I came home, my mother was very angry with me. She threw the beans out of the window and sent me to bed without supper. What can I do to make it up to my mother?

Yours truly,

Jack

Dear Jack,

I can understand why your mother was upset with you. She placed her trust in you to make a good and fair trade. You need to apologize to your mother and find a way to earn the money back. If your mother sees that you are trying to make up for letting her down, she will surely find it in her heart to forgive you. Remember, parents want the best for their children.

Good luck,

Dr. Know-It-All

P.S. If you see a tall beanstalk growing outside your window, climb it!

A. Imagine that you are Dr. Know-It-All. What advice would you offer Cinderella?

Dear Dr. Know-It-All,

This weekend, there will be a grand ball at the King's palace. The handsome prince will be choosing a bride. My mean stepmother is not allowing me to go. She is determined to have one of my stepsisters be the next queen. Between you and me, they're quite ugly and don't stand a chance. My stepmother has threatened to lock me up for the evening so that I cannot harm their chances of winning the prince's affection. This is my one chance to be free of this family. How will I ever get to the ball?

Sincerely,
Cinderella

Dear Cinderella,

_____

_____

_____

_____

_____

_____

_____

_____

_____

_____

11

B. Something is wrong with the following sentences. Use a word from the word box to correct the sentence.

market	broom	freezer	dog	tree
axe	bicycle	cat	silk	pie

1. Jack's <u>cow</u> was barking loudly. _____
2. Jack used a <u>pencil</u> to chop down the beanstalk. _____
3. Cinderella used a <u>shoe</u> to sweep the floor. _____
4. Her dress was made from blue <u>mud</u>. _____
5. The firefighter rescued our <u>giraffe</u> from the tree. _____
6. I went to the <u>library</u> to buy some fruit. _____
7. The robin built a nest in the <u>dishwasher</u>. _____
8. We kept the ice cream in the <u>closet</u>. _____
9. Michael rode his <u>guitar</u> to school. _____
10. Grandma baked a delicious <u>camera</u>. _____

C. In each row, circle three words that go together. Give a reason for your choices.

1. apple   cherry   carrot   peach

Reason _____

2. water   juice   lemonade   popcorn

Reason _____

3. taco   ice   ice cream   popsicle

Reason _____

4. truck   sled   wagon   bicycle

Reason _____

5. book   letter   magazine   carpet

Reason _____

D. Use the code to solve the following riddles.

1	2	3	4	5	6	7	8	9	10	11	12	13
A	B	C	D	E	F	G	H	I	J	K	L	M

14	15	16	17	18	19	20	21	22	23	24	25	26
N	O	P	Q	R	S	T	U	V	W	X	Y	Z

1. Why was Cinderella such a terrible baseball player?

☐☐☐   ☐☐☐   ☐   ☐☐☐☐☐☐☐
19 8 5   8 1 4   1   16 21 13 16 11 9 14

☐☐☐   ☐   ☐☐☐☐☐
6 15 18   1   3 15 1 3 8

2. What would you get if you crossed the ugly duckling with a cow?

☐☐☐☐   ☐☐☐
13 9 12 11   1 14 4

☐☐☐☐☐☐☐☐
17 21 1 3 11 5 18 19

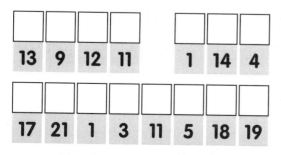

Jim Carrey is a <u>famous</u> Canadian. He has appeared in many films, but is known for his roles in The Mask, Ace Ventura: Pet Detective, Batman Forever, and How the Grinch Stole Christmas.

As a child, Jim enjoyed <u>watching</u> old comedy shows and would imitate and create a variety of characters to <u>entertain</u> his family and <u>friends</u>. He knew he wanted to be a comedian from the moment he stepped on stage for his Grade Two Christmas concert. By the time he reached Grade Seven, Jim was known as the "class clown". His talent was so impressive that his teacher allowed him fifteen minutes at the end of each day to perform for the class.

At the age of 17, Jim moved to Los Angeles where he landed his first <u>big</u> job with the Comedy Store. In no time at all, he became popular for the many <u>odd</u> and crazy characters that he played as a regular on the comedy show In Living Color. He soon realized that he wanted to be known for his <u>acting</u> and began to pursue movie roles. Jim has appeared in many <u>funny</u> movies and has been nominated for a variety of awards.

This famous Canadian's wacky sense of humour has brought laughter to audiences around the world and there's no telling what he will do next!

A. **Read the story and think about what the underlined words mean. Circle the best answer for each question.**

1. What does the word "famous" mean in the story?

   A. funny   B. popular   C. old

2. When someone is watching TV, they are _____ it.

   A. viewing   B. laughing   C. acting

3. To "entertain" means to "_____".

   A. look   B. amuse   C. eat

4. A friend is also a _____ .

   A. pal   B. enemy   C. actor

5. "Big" means "_____".

   A. tiny   B. scary   C. large

6. What does the word "odd" mean in this story?

   A. normal   B. unusual   C. funny

7. When someone is acting in a play, he is _____ .

   A. performing   B. running   C. drawing

8. "Funny" means "_____".

   A. boring   B. laughable   C. sad

B. Jim Carrey is coming to speak to your class about his life as a comedian and a movie actor. Write five questions that you would like to ask him.

1. _____

2. _____

3. _____

4. _____

5. _____

12

C. **The following sentences are about people and the jobs they do. Use a word from the word box to complete each sentence.**

dentist	comedian	reporter	stylist
mechanic	veterinarian	pilot	actor

1. A person who fixes cars is called a _____ .

2. A person who takes care of animals is a _____ .

3. A person who writes newspaper articles is called a _____ .

4. A person who performs in movies is an _____ .

5. A person who takes care of your teeth is a _____ .

6. A person who tells jokes is called a _____ .

7. A person who cuts and colours hair is called a _____ .

8. A person who controls an airplane is a _____ .

 Some words help you hear the sound when you say them. This is called **onomatopoeia**.
Example: The **hiss** of the snake frightened the children.

D. **Use each of the following sound words in an interesting sentence.**

1. bang

_____

2. crash

_____

3.  howl

_____

4.  splash

_____

E. **Comic strip writers use onomatopoeia to help the reader hear sounds. Imagine what you see when you hear the word "splat". Draw a comic to describe this sound.**

27 Mountain Road
Québec City, Quebec
March 18, 2003

Dear Uncle Marcus and Aunt Rose,

Here we are in beautiful Mount St. Anne, Quebec. I can't believe that I have learned to ski in just one day. I thought it would be much harder and scarier than it was.

First we booked lessons with our instructor and then we were fitted for boots, skis, and poles. It was difficult to walk in them, but with Dad's help, I managed to make it to meet our instructor, Jean-Luc.

Jean-Luc first taught me how to fall down and to stand back up again. We practised stopping by pointing the toes of our skis so that it looked like a slice of pizza. Then we were ready to go on the lift.

It was an amazing view, but I was getting pretty nervous about how I would make it down the hill again. Jean-Luc helped me get off the lift and took me over to the beginner hill. Together we carefully made our way down the hill. I was having so much fun, I didn't even notice when we picked up speed. Before I knew it, we had reached the bottom and I was ready to try it all over again.

Mom and Dad were really impressed to see me ski. They took lots of pictures and clapped for me at the end of the day. I can hardly wait to go back tomorrow. Maybe I'll try a bigger hill.

Love,
Angela

A. Think about an exciting place you have visited or an exciting activity you have done. Write a letter to a friend or relative about your experiences. Use Angela's letter as a model.

B. **Read the word clues. Complete the crossword puzzle by asking yourself
what you do with these things.**

Across

A. poles, boots, gloves
B. eraser, paper, pencil
C. soap, water, towel
D. novel, comic, newspaper
E. hammer, nails, wood
F. mop, broom, rag

Down

1. baseball, basketball, dart
2. skirt, sweater, shoes
3. needle, thread, material
4. bathing suit, goggles, earplugs
5. pizza, hot dogs, pasta
6. tea, juice, milk

WORD BOX

| ski | wear | throw | wash | read | drink |
| swim | sew | write | clean | build | eat |

Contractions

"It's" is a contraction. It is the short form for "it has" or "it is".

Example: **It is** time for dinner.
It's time for dinner.

"Its" means "belonging to".

Example: The baby played with **its** toy.

C. Circle the correct word in each sentence.

1. The dog was hunting for it's   its bone.

2. It's   Its very cold on the ski hill.

3. It's   Its thrilling to snowboard in Quebec.

4. The bear is looking for it's   its cub.

5. The squirrel collected it's   its acorns.

6. It's   Its been some time since we last met.

Write your own sentence using each word given.

1. it's

_____

2. Its

_____

Did you know that I am the Ruler of the Rainforest?

I can roar louder than any beast around.
> In fact, even the tigers run when they hear my call.

I can run faster than a leopard and pounce on my prey
> before my footsteps are heard.

I can swing from tree to tree without getting tired.
> The monkeys eat my dust!

I can change colour better than any chameleon around.
> I dare you to find me when I don't want to be found.

I can display my fabulous feathers prouder than any peacock.
> Even the birds of paradise want to know my secret.

I can slither through small spaces and wrap myself around a tree.
> The boa constrictor is jealous of my skills.

I can snap my jaws at the speed of light,
> leaving the crocodile with its mouth open.

I am the Ruler of the Rainforest!

 A **tall tale** is an exaggerated story. It has characters doing realistic things but in impossible ways. It includes events that could not happen in real life.

A. Match each of the following words from the passage with the proper definition.

1. ruler _____   A. extremely good or pleasant

2. roar _____   B. jump suddenly

3. beast _____   C. slide along easily

4. pounce _____   D. somebody who is in charge

5. dare _____   E. animal

6. display _____   F. make a natural growling noise

7. fabulous _____   G. challenge somebody to do something

8. slither _____   H. show something to others

B. Think about an event in your life that can be easily exaggerated. Turn this event into a tall tale that you can share with your friends.

> As I opened the basement door, a bat the size of a pterodactyl flew over my head.

My Tall Tale

_____

_____

_____

_____

_____

_____

_____

Similes

Similes compare two things using the words "like" and "as".

Examples: The jungle was hot **as** an oven.
The panther's claws were like **razors**.

C. **Match the similes. Write the letters.**

1. as fast as ☐   A. an ape

2. as hairy as ☐   B. silk

3. as fluffy as ☐   C. a cheetah

4. as cold as ☐   D. a cloud

5. as smooth as ☐   E. an iceberg

D. **Complete the following sentences with a simile.**

1. The hot air balloon was as large as _____ .

2. The dress was as beautiful as _____ .

3. The cough medicine tasted like _____ .

4. The fire alarm sounded like _____ .

5. The necklace sparkled like _____ .

Brave = Lion

A **pronoun** is a word that can take the place of a noun. **I, you**, **he**, **she**, **it**, **we**, and **they** are subject pronouns.

Examples: Justin is the fastest runner in the class.
He is the fastest runner in the class.

Bob and Mike went to the park.
They went to the park.

E.   Circle the pronoun in each sentence.

1.   She went shopping for new clothes.

2.   We are going for a hike in the forest.

3.   It has a beautiful colour.

4.   They are going out to see a movie.

5.   You look very tired.

F.   Rewrite each sentence by using a pronoun for the underlined word(s).

1.   Maria and I are going out for dinner.

_____

2.   Richard is my brother.

_____

3.   The book is very exciting to read.

_____

4.   Jennifer is the best speller in the class.

_____

5.   Larry and Michael went to watch the football game.

_____

Helen woke up to the smell of bacon and eggs. For a moment she thought she was still in her bed in Toronto but then realized that she was back in Calgary at the Four-Star Ranch, owned by her Aunt Betty and Uncle Steve. Uncle Steve picked her up at the airport the night before. It had become a yearly tradition for Helen to spend her summer vacation helping out on the ranch.

It was 6:15 a.m. and Aunt Betty was preparing breakfast for the family and wranglers who worked on the ranch. Helen jumped out of bed, pulled on her jeans, T-shirt, boots, and cowboy hat. She quickly said good morning to Aunt Betty on her way out the door. Aunt Betty knew exactly where Helen was going.

Helen was at the barn within seconds. She paused in the doorway to take in the smell of fresh hay. Suddenly, a large head popped over the stall door. Dusty, Helen's horse, stood looking at her with his mouth full of hay. He was just as excited to see her as she was to see him. Helen wrapped her arms around the big brown and white horse and gave him a hug. She could hardly wait to put a saddle on Dusty and take him for a long ride around the farm.

Helen offered Dusty an apple. As he crunched down on the delicious treat, Helen thought about all the fun things she would do with Dusty. They would herd cattle, go galloping through the fields, swim in the pond, and at the end of the day, she would groom him to make him soft and shiny. All of a sudden, she heard Aunt Betty sounding the breakfast bell. Helen raced back to the house to eat. Her summer adventure had begun.

A. Place the following "ranch" words in ABC order.

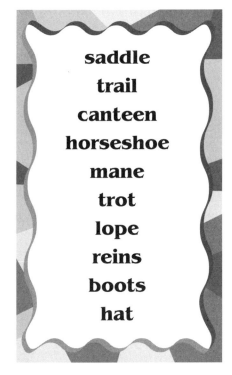

saddle
trail
canteen
horseshoe
mane
trot
lope
reins
boots
hat

1. _____

2. _____

3. _____

4. _____

5. _____

6. _____

7. _____

8. _____

9. _____

10. _____

Postcards are like short letters which are written by people on vacation. The left side is for the message and right side is for the address of the person who will get the postcard.

Here's an example of a postcard that Helen wrote to her friend in Toronto.

June 12, 2003

Howdy Simran!

    I am so glad to be back on the ranch. Dusty looks great and I was so excited to see him again. Today we went on a long ride around the farm. We helped Uncle Steve move the cattle from one pasture to another. I am exhausted but looking forward to the weekend. We will be going camping in the mountains. I'll write soon.

                        Helen

Simran Singh

12 Cherry Street

Toronto, ON

L8P 1Q4

B. Imagine that you are on a ranch just like Helen. Write a postcard to a friend telling about one of your adventures. Use some of the "ranch" words to help you.

"There", "their", and "they're" are words that sound the same but have different meanings.

"There" means "in that place".
Example: The book is over **there**.

"Their" means "belonging to them".
Example: **Their** horse is black and white.

"They're" is the short form for "They are".
Example: **They're** going camping this weekend.

C. Complete each sentence by using "there/their/they're" in the blank.

1. _____ planning to leave as soon as the horses are saddled.

2. _____ tent was set up in the meadow.

3. Please put the bale of hay over _____ .

4. We will be _____ on Saturday.

5. _____ breakfast is ready.

6. _____ here for the whole summer.

7. Helen is _____ niece.

8. Dusty stopped for a drink right _____ by the creek.

D. Use the animal words below to fill in the blanks.

kitten   *calf*   *foal*   *lamb*   *kid*   *chick*

1. A baby sheep is called a _____ .

2. A cow's baby is called a _____ .

3. A _____ is a baby cat.

4. A hen has a baby _____ .

5. A horse's baby is called a _____ .

6. A _____ is a baby goat.

A. **Read the following story. Use the words in the Word Bank to fill in the blanks.**

WORD BANK

jars   stirring   bushels   tomato   tasted

pots   picnic   recipe   sparkling   heat

It was Labour Day weekend, the most important time of the year for the Romano Family. Every year on this weekend, the entire family gathered together to make their supply of 1._____ sauce. They would make enough to last the whole year!

In the backyard, six 2._____ of fresh tomatoes stood waiting to be cleaned, cut, and boiled into a delicious sauce. Mrs. Romano was busy cleaning the huge stainless steel 3._____ in which the tomatoes would be cooked. Mr. Romano was preparing the outdoor stove which would be used to 4._____ the pots. Their two daughters, Rosemary and Pina, had the job of washing the tomatoes.

Once the tomatoes were washed, the family sat down at the 5._____ table and began to cut the tomatoes carefully into chunks. The chunks were placed into the 6._____ pots. When they had filled one, Mr. and Mrs. Romano worked together to lift the pot onto the stove. The pot was slowly heated until the tomatoes started to boil. Mrs. Romano thought about the day her mother taught her the 7._____ . She added the same special ingredients to the tomatoes and stood by the stove 8._____ and watching them turn into a thick sauce.

When the tomato sauce was ready, one important thing had to be done. The sauce had to be 9._____ . Mrs. Romano boiled some pasta and topped it with freshly made sauce. She gave a bowl to each family member and together they sampled the result of their hard work. After one taste, all four of the Romanos smiled because they knew that their tomato sauce was delicious and ready to be put into glass 10._____ .

B.   Match each of the following words with the proper definition.

1. _____ rarely

2. _____ tropical

3. _____ lazy

4. _____ survive

5. _____ environment

6. _____ pounce

7. _____ dare

8. _____ display

A. show something to others

B. challenge someone to do something

C. unwilling to do work

D. natural world where people, animals, and plants live

E. manage to stay alive

F. not very often

G. very hot and humid

H. jump suddenly

C. Place the following words in ABC order.

tomato   delicious   stove   pasta   boil   recipe

1. _____

2. _____

3. _____

4. _____

5. _____

6. _____

D. Match each word in Column A with its synonym in Column B.

Column A

1. ____ odd

2. ____ watching

3. ____ acting

4. ____ wealthy

5. ____ make

6. ____ type

Column B

A. variety

B. unusual

C. create

D. performing

E. rich

F. viewing

E. Read each word and record the number of syllables that you hear.

Syllables

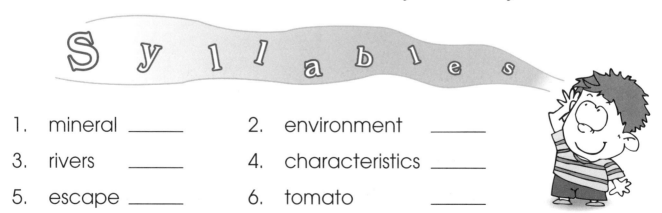

1. mineral _____

2. environment _____

3. rivers _____

4. characteristics _____

5. escape _____

6. tomato _____

F. In each row, circle three words that go together. Give a reason for your choices.

1.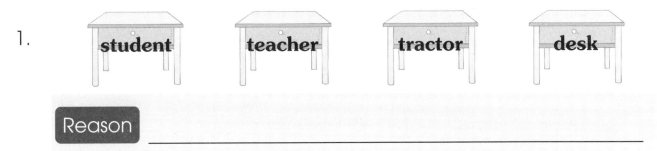

   student   teacher   tractor   desk

   Reason _____

2.

   pizza   taco   hamburger   blocks

   Reason _____

3.

   peas   lemon   carrots   spinach

   Reason _____

G. Correct the following sentences with the given words.

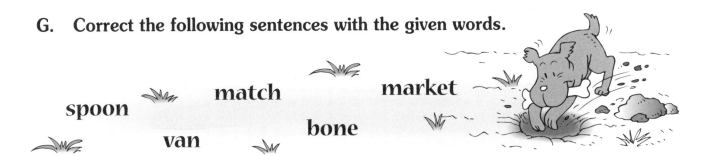

spoon   match   market
bone
van

1. She used a <u>tomato</u> to light the fire.   _____

2. Mrs. Romano used a <u>hammer</u> to stir the sauce.   _____

3. We went to the <u>library</u> to buy our tomatoes.   _____

4. Mom drove the <u>vacuum</u> to the plaza.   _____

5. The dog buried its <u>telephone</u> in the backyard.   _____

H. **Write the plurals for the following words.**

1. tourist _____
2. lunch _____
3. country _____
4. fox _____
5. address _____
6. wish _____
7. goose _____
8. woman _____

Five mice

I. **Circle the correct word in each sentence.**

1. (It's, Its) very hot in Jamaica.

2. The baby is looking for (it's, its) toy.

3. (Their, They're) going to the airport to pick up Grandma.

4. Please put the jars over (there, their).

5. Rosemary is (there, their) daughter.

J. **Replace the underlined words with pronouns. Write them in the boxes.**

1. <u>Rosemary</u> is going to the store to buy tomatoes.

2. <u>Sabrina and Josie</u> are best friends.

3. <u>Gary</u> is an excellent artist.

4. <u>Rosemary and I</u> are planning a party for Rob.

5. <u>The toy</u> was under the bed.

K. Complete the following sentences.

1. A young cat is called a _____ .

2. A young horse is called a _____ .

3. A young goat is called a _____ .

4. A young sheep is called a _____ .

L. Match each idiom with its correct meaning.

1. Hold your horses. _____   A. Be patient and wait.

2. I have butterflies in my _____   B. Stop acting silly.
   stomach.

3. Quit horsing around. _____   C. I was afraid.

4. I was shaking in my boots. _____   D. I'm nervous.

M. Complete the following sentences with the given words.

pilot   veterinarian   comedian   dentist

1. A person who takes care of your teeth is called a _____ .

2. A person who controls an airplane is called a _____ .

3. A person who takes care of animals is called a _____ .

4. A person who tells jokes is called a _____ .

Welcome

Language Games

1

Dolly is trying to catch the ball. Colour her path following the letters in the words "throw and catch".

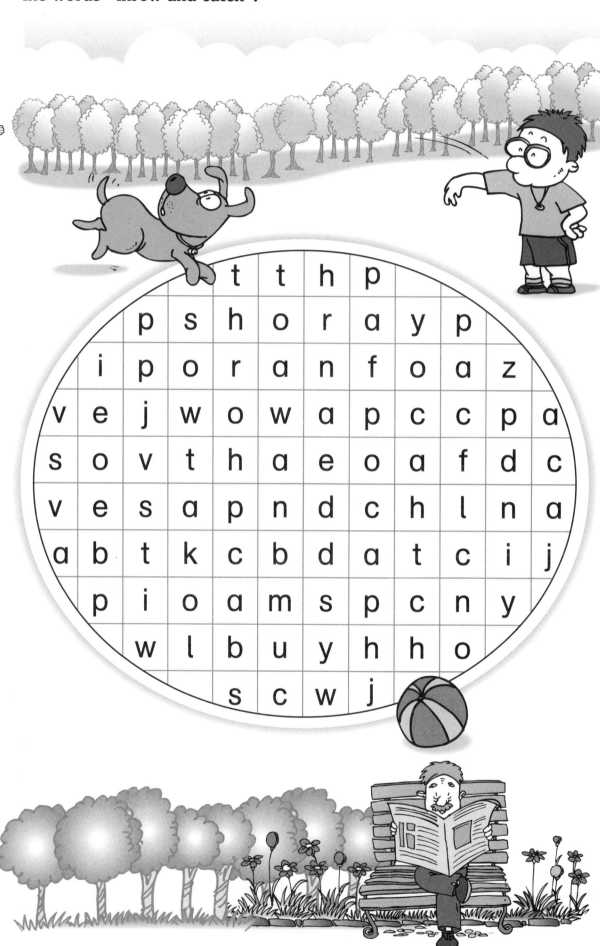

	t	t	h	p			
p	s	h	o	r	a	y	p
i	p	o	r	a	n	f	o	a	z
v	e	j	w	o	w	a	p	c	c	p	a
s	o	v	t	h	a	e	o	a	f	d	c
v	e	s	a	p	n	d	c	h	l	n	a
a	b	t	k	c	b	d	a	t	c	i	j
p	i	o	a	m	s	p	c	n	y
w	l	b	u	y	h	h	o
	s	c	w	j			

2 The animals are making different sounds. Complete what they say.

squeal   bark   trumpet   hoot   squeak
quack   mew   crow   roar

1. I _____ .

2. I _____ .

3. I _____ .

4. I _____ .

5. I _____ .

6. I _____ .

7. I _____ .

8. I _____ .

9. I _____ .

3 Simon the Squirrel phoned home and left a message. Follow and colour the buttons under the ♡ to get his message.

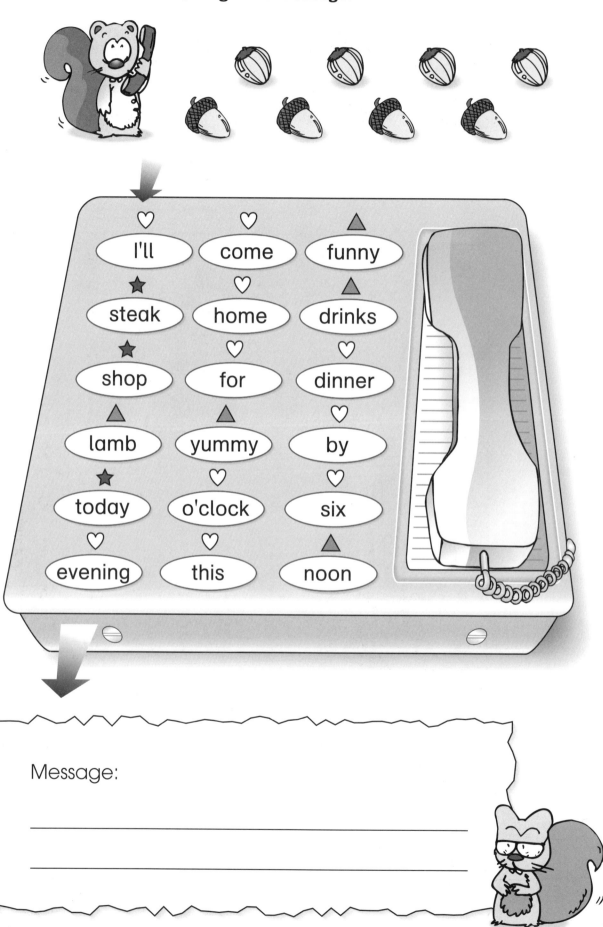

Message: _____

_____

_____

4 It's near Christmas. Help Little Fairy circle the "Christmas" words in the word search.

presents   holly   lights   snow
Rudolph   reindeer   decorations
tinsel   party   Noel   carols   sleigh
angels   Santa Claus

R	u	d	o	l	p	h	l	y	c	p
a	n	e	l	w	a	t	i	s	l	a
n	e	c	p	o	n		g	h	c	r
g	h	o	l	l	y	p	h	m	a	t
e	p	r	e	s	e	n	t	s	r	y
l	N	a		c	l	d	s	n	o	w
s	o	t	i	n	s	e	l	t	l	
r	e	i	n	d	e	e	r	i	s	n
a	l	o	w	k	l	i	t	g	o	d
S	a	n	t	a		C	l	a	u	s
n	d	s	l	e	i	g	h	t	u	s

5

Follow the path that forms "Halloween" words. Colour what you can find.

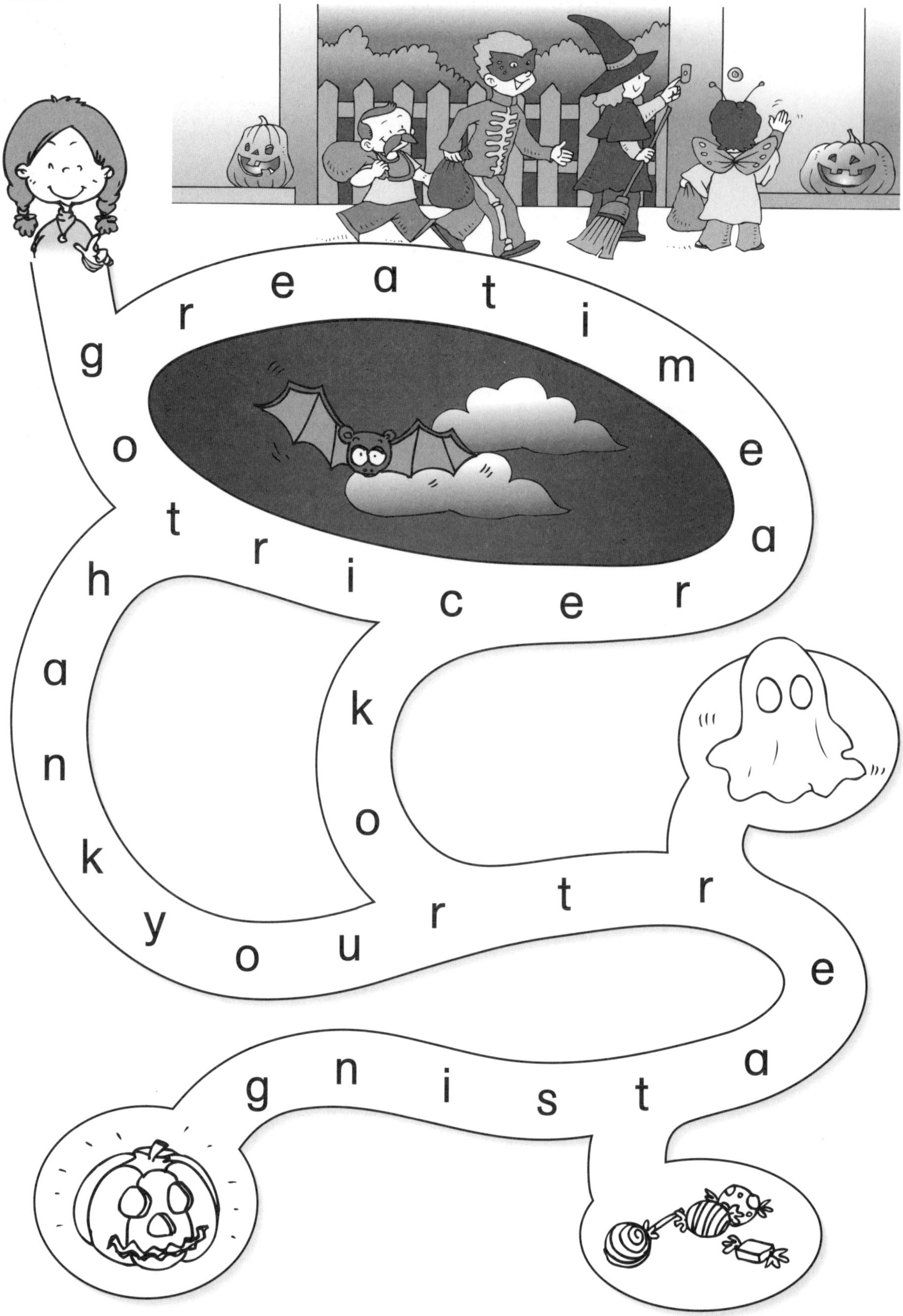

g r e a t i m e a

g o t r i c e r

h a n k y o u r t r e a

k o

g n i s t

Halloween

6 Look at the pictures. Complete the Fruit Crossword Puzzle.

7

Draw lines to match the three columns of puzzle pieces.

1.   sweet  ice

2.  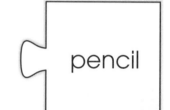 cold  pencil

3.   sharp  lollipop

4. 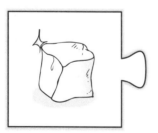  heavy 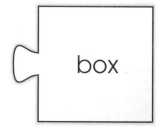 tea

5. 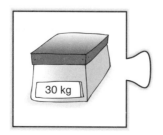  hot 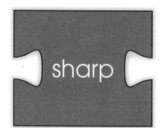 box

8 Write what the magic carpets say.

1.

how   am   to   I   fly
eager   learn   to

_____

_____

2.

say   fly   "magic"   when
I   you   will   .

_____

_____

3.

but   know   I   fly   can't
I   magic.

_____

_____

9

Circle the "animal" words in the Animal Word Search.

Animal
Word Search

chimpanzee   crocodile
raccoon   cheetah
tiger   skunk   bear
beaver   penguin
giraffe   zebra
kangaroo   lion
caribou

g	o	l	c	v	b	s	k	u	n	k	i
n	c	h	e	e	t	a	h	g	m	h	d
l	f	a	y	r	j	v	c	l	k	c	x
i	k	g	i	r	a	f	f	e	p	h	e
o	a	h	k	a	p	e	n	g	u	i	n
n	n	d	b	c	a	u	c	i	t	m	c
b	g	e	m	c	h	x	o	w	a	p	a
d	a	j	g	o	k	t	e	b	q	a	r
c	r	o	c	o	d	i	l	e	s	n	i
j	o	z	f	n	t	g	m	a	f	z	b
e	o	a	o	d	z	e	b	r	a	e	o
k	b	e	a	v	e	r	h	i	b	e	u

10 Circle the present Little Jill gets from Santa Claus by following the three-syllable words.

Christmas

glittering   mistletoe   festival

carol   tree   feast   decorate

present   Noel   gathering   holiday

tinsel   merry   family

JIGSAW

VIDEO GAME

11

Read the clues and complete the crossword puzzle.

1. This unusual pet has a long slender body and feeds on small rodents.
3. If your pet gets lost, you try to _____ it as quickly as possible.
5. You can have lots of _____ with your pets.
6. Pets are like us; they need food and _____ .
8. Many people think that cats can see in the _____ .
9. Dogs can _____ sounds that human beings can't.

Down

1. The long stiff hairs that grow near a cat's mouth
2. Pet food sometimes comes in a _____ (can).
3. This keeps cats warm in winter.
4. Some dogs, such as spaniels, have _____ ears.
5. We should _____ our pets about the same time each day.
7. A pet dog can be a _____ and companion.

12 Draw an animal that lives in each home.

cave

nest

doghouse

hive

stable

pond

13 Mother Hen wants to bake a yummy pizza for her family. Follow and colour the slices with toppings that she can put on the dough to help her get to the oven.

pepperoni

clip

ice

ham

chalk

olive

tomato

paper

red pepper

bug

rock

cheese

onion

soil

rubber

mushroom

14

Draw lines to match the animal mothers with their babies.

1

duckling

2

owlet

3

lamb

4

puppy

5

kitten

6

chick

7

cub

8

piglet

9

kid

10

calf

15 There are many shapes in the Shape Kingdom. Circle the words in the word search.

SHAPES

triangle	trapezoid	pentagon
circle	square	hexagon
octagon	star	rectangle

o	p	e	t	a	m	h	g	n	t	a	c
e	g	t	r	a	p	e	z	o	i	d	k
c	o	l	e	n	p	x	a	c	t	a	g
c	i	r	c	l	e	a	n	t	r	t	b
r	p	e	t	a	s	g	u	a	e	r	o
s	q	u	a	r	e	o	a	g	o	i	r
t	u	i	n	g	e	n	g	o	y	a	j
a	e	t	g	n	o	x	d	n	t	n	e
r	a	z	l	i	a	g	n	i	a	g	u
e	h	p	e	n	t	a	g	o	n	l	m
c	t	d	i	m	u	p	e	d	l	e	q
h	n	a	l	s	f	e	d	p	i	v	t

16

Matt the Magician is doing magic. Show how he changes a cup to a mug by changing one letter in the word each time.

C	U	P

1.

2.

3.

4.

5.

6.

17 Dr. Wrights can lead you out of the ancient tomb. Follow what he says and colour the path out.

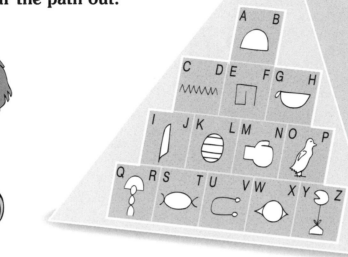

This Egyptian tomb is awesome!

18 Look at the pictures. Write the compound words.

1. + =

2. + =

3. +  =

4. +  =

5. + =

6. + =

7. + =

8. + =

9.  +  =

19 Help Marcia find her lost rabbit by following the route with the words that rhyme with "park".

hark   lark

bark   lack   clock

shark

work   dark

dock   make

back   spark

pick   mark   shock

bake   pack

park   pork

Read the clues and complete the crossword puzzle on nature.

Across

A. Something white and soft falling from the sky

B. Coloured light seen in the night sky near the North Pole

C. High hill

D. Distant planets twinkling in the night sky

E. Moving air

Down

1. Another name for "shooting star"

2. It warms our Earth.

3. Salt water in which people like to swim

4. Colourful arch formed in the sky

5. The biggest and brightest object in the night sky

6. Large area of water surrounded by land

N A T U R E

1. Nunavut, Canada's Newest Territory

A.
1. The Yukon and the Northwest Territories.
2. Iqualuit.
3. About 25,000 people.
4. Because much of Nunavut is above the Arctic Circle.
5. About 9 months.
6. It stays frozen all year round.
7. Snowmobiles and planes.
8. Inuktitut.
9. On dogsleds.
10. The seal.

B. Person : baby ; citizen ; player ; owner ; manager ; child
Place : school ; farm ; room ; lake ; road ; park
Thing : leaf ; sweater ; desk ; stick ; pen ; truck
Idea : effort ; help ; task ; lie ; promise ; joy
Proper Noun : Mrs. Jones ; Moon River ; CN Tower ; Backstreet Boys ; Mt. Albert ; Dr. Smith

C.
1. B   2. C   3. T   4. P
5. Q   6. R   7. X   8. J

D. (Answers will vary.)

2. What Makes up Our Universe?

A.
1. B   2. F   3. D   4. C
5. A   6. E

B. (Suggested answers)
1. There was an explosion in the universe that sent millions of particles out in space. Some of these particles crashed into one another and stuck together forming a solar system.
2. The Milky Way got its name because it looks like a white stream of light.

C.
1. shot   2. fell
3. missed   4. cheered
5. raised

D. (Suggested answers)
1. gathered   2. swung
3. played   4. helped
5. bounced   6. called

E.
1. plate ; long   2. duck ; short
3. come ; short   4. may ; long
5. stone ; long   6. toe ; long
7. pop ; short   8. clue ; long
9. throw ; long

F.
1. It is a beautiful day today.

2. Yes, it is. Shall we go outside?
3. Let's go to the park.
4. Would you like to come too?
5. Thank you for asking me to join you.
6. Look. There's John. Let's ask him to come along.
7. I'd love to go to the park. Shall I bring a soccer ball?

3. Are We Alone in the Universe?

A.
1. sun   2. water
3. warmth   4. 100
5. extra-terrestrial   6. spaceships
7. captured   8. harmed

B. (Answers will vary.)

C.
1. aliens'   2. alien's
3. boys'   4. girls'
5. Jim's   6. children's
7. coaches'   8. James's
9. children's   10. girl's
11. girls'   12. Julie's

D.
1. hid   2. hug
3. cut   4. us
5. bit   6. rip
7. tap   8. pin
9. at   10. mad
11. cub   12. fir

4. The Simpsons (1)

A.
1. F   2. F   3. T   4. T
5. F   6. T   7. T   8. F

B. (Suggested answers)
1. It gave him ideas for characters and situations.
2. He has good imagination and artistic skills.

C.
1. I   2. He ; him
3. we ; it   4. We ; them
5. me ; my

D.
1. We   2. I
3. He   4. She
5. me

Section 1 Answers

E. Crossword A

Across: A. WEST, B. MAGAZINES
Down: 1. WEALTH, 2. WIFE, 3. DREW

Crossword B

Across: A. CARTOONS, B. SCHOOL
Down: 1. BY, 2. PPULAR, 3. COAST, 1. BUY

4. Always stay in the shallow end of the pool if you are a beginning swimmer.
5. Check below the water surface in rivers and lakes.
6. Wear a lifejacket in a boat.

B. (Writing will vary.)

C. 1. dark ; young   2. warm ; winter
3. Wild ; natural   4. Old ; good
5. careful ; busy ; slippery

D. 1. furry   2. icy
3. cold ; white   4. excited ; birthday
5. Happy

E. 1. E   2. G   3. H   4. A
5. B   6. C   7. D   8. I
9. F

F. 1A. dangerous   B. supervised
C. enjoyable
2. investigate

5 The Simpsons (2)

A. 1. B   2. A   3. C   4. A
5. C   6. B   7. A   8. C
9. A   10. B

B. 2. Joanne dropped her book.
3. Fido is its name.
4. The hat is hers.
5. That book is yours.
6. This house is mine.
7. The toys are theirs.
8. The new shoes are his.

C. 1. beaten ; sweeten
2. gift ; lift
3. hotter ; swatter ; Potter
4. snore ; chore ; store
5. liver ; river ; sliver ; shiver
6. brow ; chow ; now ; plough
7. brew ; flew ; glue ; shoe
8. crept ; wept ; swept ; slept

D. (Writing will vary.)

6 Water Safety

A. (Suggested answers)
1. Swim with a buddy.
2. Never swim at a beach with no lifeguards.
3. Do not run around the pool area.

7 Accidental Inventions

A. (Suggested answer)
When something is needed, it will be invented.

B. (Suggested answers)
1. Because he turned an accidental invention into a business.
2. It only happened when an ice cream vendor ran out of cups and needed something to serve the ice cream.
3. (Answers will vary.)

C. (Some answers may vary.)
1. high   2. skilfully
3. directly   4. quickly
5. cleverly   6. swiftly
7. loudly   8. immediately
9. loudly

D. 2. meet   3. meat
4. team   5. coat
6. stay   7. sail
8. bait   9. stray
10. toast   11. friend

8 The Second Most Popular Drink in the World

A. 1. A   2. A   3. B   4. A
5. C   6. A

B. 1. The girls | played volleyball.
2. His parents | went out.

3. They | watched television together.
4. The fast runner | won the race.
5. The first person in the gym | turned on the lights.

C. (Answers will vary.)

D. (Answers will vary.)

E.
1. bleed
2. clues
3. chick
4. sleepy
5. trick
6. crab
7. brick
8. wash

F. (Answers will vary.)

9 Fossils – The Link to the Dinosaur

A.
1. B
2. A
3. C
4. A
5. B

B.
1. Dinosaurs roamed the world many years ago.
2. Summer holidays are finally here.
3. We won the game.
4. The teacher gave the pupils a test.
5. He ate two scoops of ice cream.
6. It rained all day long.

C.
1. B
2. C
3. D
4. A

D.
1. spread
2. stream
3. scream
4. threw
5. straw
6. square
7. street
8. spring

E.

							2		
	1						S		
	S						C		
A	S	T	R	A	W	B	E	R	R	Y
	R						U		
	E						B		
	T								
B	S	C	R	A	M	B	L	E	
	H								

Progress Test 1

A.
1. F
2. T
3. T
4. T
5. F
6. F
7. T
8. T
9. F
10. T
11. F
12. F
13. F
14. F
15. T
16. F
17. F
18. T
19. F
20. F
21. T
22. T
23. F
24. T
25. F

B. Noun : morning ; school ; time ; playground ; teams
Pronoun : It ; they
Verb : was ; reported ; waited ; ran ; picked ; started

Adjective : bright ; sunny ; first ; happy ; homework ; furious
Adverb : again ; anxiously ; quickly

C.
1. his
2. Jane's
3. waitress's
4. boys'
5. Susie's
6. mine

D.
1. his
2. their
3. our
4. his

E.
1. happy
2. sad
3. cold
4. courageous
5. funny
6. terrible
7. dangerous
8. quick

F.
1. quickly
2. merrily
3. smoothly
4. around
5. nicely
6. creatively
7. mindfully
8. securely

G.
1. Winter is our longest season.
2. Cats and dogs seldom get along.
3. The hockey game went into overtime.
4. How many days are there in a school year?
5. The storm left everything covered with snow.

H.
1. B
2. D
3. A
4. C

I.
1. long
2. short
3. short
4. long
5. long
6. long
7. long
8. short
9. long
10. long

J. (Answers will vary.)

K.
1. slush
2. cream
3. stream
4. chalk
5. trip
6. sneaky
7. scrap
8. terrible
9. throw
10. swat

10 Are You Superstitious?

A.
1. F
2. T
3. T
4. T
5. F
6. F
7. T
8. T
9. T
10. T

B.
1. B
2. C
3. A

C.
1. Take your seats before the game begins. ; imperative
2. Which team is winning so far? ; interrogative
3. The pitcher has struck out three batters. ; declarative
4. The bases are loaded. ; declarative
5. Wow, what a great catch! ; exclamatory

6. Is the runner fast enough to steal a base? ; interrogative
D. (Answers will vary.)
E. 1. basketball   2. homework
3. snowman   4. playground
5. photograph   6. airport
7. bedroom   8. overflow
9. outside   10. nightmare
F. GRAVEYARD

11   Babies of the Arctic

A. 1. For two years.
2. Polar bears and killer whales.
3. They form a circle with their tusks facing outward.
4. For ten days.
5. Because it cannot see, hear, or walk.
6. She smothers the cub in her coat and feeds it warm milk.
7. They have either fur or fat to protect them against the cold.
B. (Answers will vary.)
C. 1. ships ; 1   2. foxes ; 2
3. wives ; 4   4. knives ; 4
5. potatoes ; 5   6. geese ; 7
7. tomatoes ; 5   8. boots ; 1
9. feet ; 7   10. halves ; 4
11. enemies ; 3   12. keys ; 1
13. skis ; 1   14. skies ; 3
D. 1. H   2. J   3. G   4. B
5. C   6. A   7. E   8. D
9. F   10. I
E. 1. surviving   2. believable
3. appearance   4. uninhabited

12   The Origin of Gum Chewing

A.

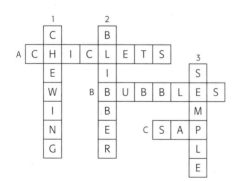

B. (Answers will vary.)

C. 1. carried ; will carry
2. run ; will run
3. thought ; will think
4. fight ; fought
5. tried ; will try
6. swim ; swam
D. 1. played
2. will try
3. worked / will work
4. will fly
5. walks / will walk / walked
6. will take
7. goes / went
8. met
E. 1. been   2. father
3. would   4. pale
5. week   6. hare
7. brake   8. flour
9. maid   10. wait
11. hole   12. write

13   Trick or Treat

A. 1. B   2. D   3. A   4. E
5. C
B. (Suggested answers)
1. As punishment for playing tricks on the devil.
2. They would go back to their old homes before they died.
3. When they see a jack-o'-lantern on porches and windows.
C. 1. she'll   2. he'd
3. we're   4. you're
5. weren't   6. who's
7. didn't   8. hasn't
9. I'm   10. that's
11. haven't   12. wouldn't
13. isn't   14. there's
D. (Answers will vary.)
E. (Writing will vary.)

14   Understanding the Food Chain

A. 1. the lettuce   2. the slug
3. the beetle   4. the shrew
5. the owl
B. (Suggested answers)
1. They provide energy for the first link in the food chain.

2. It means to pass energy from one thing to another.
3. It can fly and no animals prey on it.
4. We would be placed at the top of the food chain.
5. (Suggested answers)
   A. lion   B. polar bear
   C. tiger
C. My Trip to England

   My name is Billy Henderson. I live at 723 Main St. My dad is a doctor and his patients call him Dr. Henderson. This summer we are going on a holiday to England to visit my aunt, Rita. Rita lives near the Thames River. We are going to visit Buckingham Palace while we are there. Our flight is booked on British Airways and we will land at Heathrow Airport. We are leaving on August 11, and returning on September 3. While we are away, our neighbour, Mrs. Watson, will look after our dog, Scamp.

D.

		2		3		
A	u	n	h	a	p	p	y
		a		l		
B s	e	a	s	C a	d	d
		t		t		4
D s	t	a	y	E e	n	d
a						r
w						o
						p

15   The Biggest Pest of the Summer

A. 1. F   2. T   3. T   4. F
   5. F   6. F   7. F   8. T
   9. F   10. F   11. T   12. T
B. (Answers will vary.)
C. 1. are   2. is
   3. come   4. were
   5. is   6. was
   7. taken   8. like
D. 1. arrive   2. are
   3. is   4. comes
   5. is   6. were
E. 1. enemy   2. play
   3. safe   4. hard
   5. calm   6. ruin
   7. empty
F. 1. ugly   2. serious

3. regular   4. dull
5. wild   6. weak

16   The Mystery of Migration

A. 1. B   2. A   3. B   4. C
   5. A   6. B
B. 1. The happy boy ran quickly.
   2. The howling wind blew furiously.
   3. The talented grade three students sang the songs loudly.
   4. The exciting game was finished early.
   5. John, the oldest boy in the class, was late again.
C. (Answers will vary.)
D. (Suggested answers)
   1. He led me all over the place.
   2. If you are the first, you will win.
   3. We tried to convince the teacher to give us less homework.
   4. When she lost her cat, she was sad.
   5. The grade three students were in trouble for breaking the window.
   6. My dad was very angry when he got a flat tire.
E. (Answers will vary.)
   1. (Meaning : very special)
   2. (Meaning : tell everything)
   3. (Meaning : going crazy)

17   Mary Kate and Ashley Olsen

A. 1. nine months   2. "Two of a Kind"
   3. Michelle Tanner   4. "Full House"
   5. "Our First Video"   6. ten dollars
   7. Trent ; Elizabeth   8. California
B. (Writing will vary.)
C.

B	U	I	L	D	I	N	G	J	K
H	A	R	M	F	U	L	Q	W	E
A	S	M	P	I	T	I	F	U	L
P	A	F	T	N	E	W	E	S	T
P	R	I	C	E	L	E	S	S	R
I	R	T	O	S	S	I	N	G	A
N	O	N	H	T	R	V	U	L	P
E	V	E	N	T	F	U	L	Z	P
S	E	S	A	D	N	E	S	S	E
S	N	S	T	O	P	P	E	R	D

D.   (Order may vary.)
1. happy   2. harm
3. fine   4. new
5. pity   6. price
7. event   8. trap
9. toss   10. sad
11. stop   12. build

Progress Test 2

A.   1. B   2. C   3. A   4. C
5. B   6. B   7. C   8. A
9. A   10. B   11. B   12. C
13. A   14. A   15. B   16. C
17. A   18. B   19. B   20. C
21. A

B.   1. Mr. Jones was also known as Dr. Jones when he was at Toronto General Hospital.
2. Linda and Lauren attended Willow Avenue Public School.
3. They took a canoe trip on the Niagara River near Quebec City.
4. We all read the Harry Potter books by J.K. Rowling.

C.   1. ships   2. potatoes
3. feet   4. knives
5. foxes   6. halves
7. wives   8. skis

D.   1. How are you feeling today? ; interrogative
2. Today is Monday. ; declarative
3. Look out ! ; exclamatory
4. Sit down and be quiet. ; imperative

E.   1. she'll   2. we'll
3. didn't   4. haven't
5. wouldn't   6. that's

F.   1. will arrive   2. walked
3. jumps / will jump   4. worked

G.   1. are   2. were
3. go   4. take
5. are

H.   1. joyous   2. dull
3. sluggish   4. tiny
5. silent   6. weak
7. careless

I.   1. rude   2. empty
3. smooth   4. dry
5. skinny   6. dull
7. healthy

J.   (Order may vary.)
1. fireplace   2. strawberry
3. photograph   4. baseball
5. bathroom   6. forehead
7. handwriting   8. notebook
9. pillowcase   10. grapefruit
11. outside   12. downtown
13. everyone   14. mailbox

K.   1. E   2. D   3. A   4. B
5. C

1 Nouns

A. (Answers will vary.)
1. trees
2. sun
3. swings
4. see-saw
5. flowers
6. bench

B. (Individual drawing)

C. 1. Fruits
2. Head
3. Mouth
4. Animals
5. Colours
6. Numbers

D. (Suggested answers)
1b. bat   c. hat   d. mat   e. rat
2b. hand   c. land   d. sand   e. wand
3b. brain   c. grain   d. train

E. 1. girls ; party
2. cars ; lot
3. set ; box
4. jacket
5. candle ; hours

F. 1. mountain
2. stadium
3. city
4. drug store
5. supermarket
6. painting
7. boy

G. 1. Jennifer
2. CN Tower ; Toronto
3. Parliament Buildings ; Ottawa
4. Teddy ; Bellriver School
5. China
6. Spice Girls
7. Tokyo ; Japan
8. Disneyland

H. (Answers will vary.)

2 Noun Plurals

A. (Any order)
2. 3 computers
3. 10 desks
4. 8 chairs
5. 4 windows
6. 2 blackboards
7. 3 books
8. 12 pencils
9. 6 pictures

B. 1. tax – taxes
2. wish – wishes
3. church – churches
4. bus – buses
5. bush – bushes
6. dish – dishes
7. inch – inches
8. dress – dresses
9. peach – peaches
10. ash – ashes
11. lunch – lunches
12. fox – foxes

C. 1. cities
2. bunnies
3. babies
4. bodies
5. ladies
6. countries
7. stories
8. factories
9. families
10. candies

D. 1. stories
2. families
3. bunnies
4. babies
5. bodies
6. cities
7. candies
8. factories

E. 1. shoe ; shoes
2. cookie ; cookies
3. doctor ; doctors
4. glass ; glasses

5. bee ; bees
6. uncle ; uncles
7. wish ; wishes
8. bus ; buses

3 Irregular Plural Nouns

A. 1. tooth – teeth
2. child – children
3. deer – deer
4. salmon – salmon
5. woman – women
6. reindeer – reindeer
7. sheep – sheep
8. man – men
9. foot – feet
10. ox – oxen

B. 1. wives
2. calves
3. wolves
4. leaves
5. knives
6. halves
7. yourselves
8. shelves
9. lives
10. elves

C.

t	u	p	r	q	x	f	m
o	k	g	h	y	m	t	s
j	m	d	i	c	e	j	l
x	f	r	n	h	d	p	f
b	j	l	o	l	i	k	c
t	k	i	c	b	u	n	v
w	i	f	e	g	m	i	p
f	c	e	r	d	w	f	s
h	r	m	o	u	s	e	k
d	n	v	s	c	a	r	f

j	d	g	m	l	b	r	p
w	i	v	e	s	r	h	f
f	c	q	d	k	t	i	z
k	e	s	i	c	h	n	x
n	k	c	a	w	j	o	d
i	b	a	g	m	q	c	r
v	n	r	l	i	v	e	s
e	d	v	f	c	s	r	y
s	h	e	w	e	u	o	g
c	r	s	l	p	f	s	v

(Any order)
1. wife ; wives
2. dice ; dice
3. life ; lives
4. scarf ; scarves
5. knife ; knives
6. rhinoceros ; rhinoceros
7. mouse ; mice
8. medium ; media

D. 1. rhinoceros
2. lives
3. mice
4. dice
5. sheep
6. knives
7. wives
8. Children ; deer
9. feet

4 Pronouns and Articles

A. 1. They
2. He
3. We

B. 1. She
2. We
3. We
4. she / we
5. it
6. We
7. We
8. He

C. 1. The bus is picking them up at the station.
2. Michael can go to the movies with her.
3. Patricia is taking it to him.
4. Mom has given us some chocolate.

D. 1. us
2. She
3. us
4. Her

E. 1. a
2. an
3. an
4. a
5. a
6. an

7. an   8. a   9. a
10. a
F. 1. A ; a   2. An   3. A ; the
4. A ; a   5. An ; a ; a   6. A
G. 1. a   2. It   3. the
4. the   5. an   6. The
7. an   8. its   9. a
10. the   11. it   12. They
13. The   14. the   15. It
16. I

5 Verbs

A. swings ; skips ; runs ; talks ; cycles ; climbs ; throws
B. 1. barked   2. opened
3. walked   4. climbed
5. pushed   6. cooked
C. 1. coloured   2. fished
3. crawled   4. jumped
5. sailed   6. touched
7. smiled   8. played
D. (Any order)
1. feed ; fed   2. make ; made
3. throw ; threw   4. lose ; lost
5. try ; tried   6. run ; ran
7. swim ; swam   8. tear ; tore
9. blow ; blew   10. drink ; drank
E. 1. went   2. saw
3. did   4. bought
5. takes   6. held
7. left   8. stood
9. caught   10. drinks

6 "Being" Verbs

A. 1. am   2. are
3. is   4. are
5. is   6. are
7. are   8. are
9. are   10. are
B. 1. were   2. was
3. was   4. were
5. were   6. was
7. were
C. 1. has   2. has
3. had   4. had
5. had   6. has
7. has   8. have
9. has   10. had
11. had   12. had
13. had
D. 1. were   2. was
3. had   4. was
5. were   6. had

7. am   8. is
9. have

7 Sentence Types

A. (Answers will vary.)
B. 1. How many planets are there?
2. Which planet do we live on?
3. Which planet is the farthest from the Earth?
4. Where does the Earth travel?
5. How many rings does Saturn have?
6. What actually is the Sun?
7. What is your favourite planet?
C. (Answers will vary.)
D. 1. C   2. C   3. NC
4. C   5. C   6. NC
7. C   8. NC
E. 1. E   2. NE   3. E
4. E   5. NE   6. NE
7. E
F. (Answers will vary.)

Progress Test 1

A.   Our (family) took a (trip) to <u>Toronto</u> last <u>July</u>. We flew to <u>Pearson International Airport</u> and from there, we took a (cab) to our downtown (hotel). The (name) of our (hotel) was the <u>Royal York</u>. It was very nice and very close to so many (attractions).

On our first (day), we went to the <u>Hockey Hall of Fame</u> and saw all of our favourite hockey (players') (memorabilia). We also went to the <u>SkyDome</u> for a (tour). On our second (day), we went up to the observation (deck) of the <u>CN Tower</u> and we had (dinner) at a fun (restaurant) called "<u>The Old Spaghetti Factory</u>".

What a great (trip) we had!

B. 1. eggs   2. boys
3. dresses   4. coats
5. hearts   6. years
7. flowers   8. peaches
9. fences   10. brushes
C.

b	d	f	h	j	n	l	b	o	q	g
r	a	n	t	o	p	q	u	k	r	l
b	e	n	c	h	e	s	s	i	g	a
u	s	v	t	b	a	u	h	s	p	s
s	k	m	a	t	c	h	e	s	o	s
e	w	c	m	d	h	v	s	e	h	e
s	y	b	o	x	e	s	f	s	j	s
z	f	o	x	e	s	e	u	w	s	f
b	r	a	n	c	h	e	s	i	l	x

D. 1. <u>Mom</u> baked (muffins) for <u>breakfast</u>.
2. Alice has five (brothers) and a <u>sister</u>.
3. Andrew got new (skis) for his <u>birthday</u>.
4. Petra put the (puzzles) in the <u>rack</u> on the <u>table</u>.
5. The two (houses) are near the <u>road</u>.
6. There are lots of (apples) in that <u>tree</u>.

E. 1. He ; it   2. It
3. She ; it   4. He ; her

F. 1. the   2. a ; the
3. the ; the   4. a / the ; a / the
5. The ; a

G. 1. raced   2. planned
3. floated   4. played
5. kicked   6. wish

H. 1. added   2. pulled
3. played   4. walked
5. opened   6. locked

I. 1. crawl   2. sew
3. push   4. bark
5. cook   6. want

J. 1. eat – ate   2. sleep – slept
3. hold – held   4. feed – fed
5. take – took   6. throw – threw
7. give – gave   8. catch – caught

K. 1. went   2. buy
3. drank   4. fought
5. bought   6. leaves

L. 1. are   2. am
3. are   4. are
5. is   6. are
7. are   8. are
9. is

M. 1. has   2. have
3. has   4. have
5. have

N. 1. The television – was   2. Boys – were
3. A cup – was   4. A zebra – was
5. Balloons – were

8   Punctuation and Capitalization

A. 1. !   2. ?   3. .   4. .
5. ?   6. !   7. ?   8. .
9. ?   10. !   11. !   12. .

B. 1. is not – isn't   2. were not – weren't
3. has not – hasn't   4. do not – don't
5. did not – didn't   6. have not – haven't
7. cannot – can't   8. could not – couldn't
9. would not – wouldn't   10. was not – wasn't
11. should not – shouldn't

C. 1. The Three Little Pigs
2. Frog and Toad Are Friends
3. Curious George and the Man with the Yellow Hat
4. The Princess and the Pea
5. I Have to Go
6. Love You Forever

D. (Answers will vary.)

E.

c	b	f	j	m	u	s	d	h	y	k	z	x
m	t	s	o	r	m	d	r	e	s	g	c	h
j	t	h	e	b	o	r	r	o	w	e	r	s
l	i	r	u	n	n	p	q	a	d	i	l	k
b	o	e	b	h	s	c	s	m	u	v	o	b
g	q	k	w	a	t	l	a	n	t	i	s	f
v	d	t	l	y	e	g	x	s	v	o	c	r
s	o	a	b	f	r	u	h	b	i	a	q	v
c	w	n	g	v	s	j	h	z	p	y	w	d
v	l	r	c	h	i	c	k	a	d	e	e	z
i	s	w	n	l	n	r	l	g	t	m	w	h
m	e	x	p	t	c	k	e	y	v	a	j	p

(Any order)
1. Atlantis   2. Shrek
3. Owl   4. Chickadee
5. The Borrowers   6. Monsters, Inc.

9   Adjectives

A. 1.   2.
3.   4.
5.  blue   6. purple

B. (Individual drawings)
1. four   2. eight
3. two   4. one
5. three

C. 1. juicy   2. sticky
3. sweet   4. hot
5. rotten   6. creamy
7. soft   8. hard

D. (Answers will vary.)

E. 1. taller   2. biggest
3. smallest   4. shorter
5. bigger

10 Parts of Sentences

A. 1. animals   2. tree
   3. coconut   4. oranges
   5. Candles
B. 1. The dog – chewed the bone.
   2. The mail carrier – delivered the letter.
   3. The nurse – gave her a needle.
   4. The teacher – taught the lesson.
   5. The hockey player – scored a goal.
   6. The zoo keeper – fed the animals.
C. 1. Pioneers   2. Log cabins
   3. Vegetables   4. Clothes
   5. Canoes
D. 1. A banana   2. Igloos
   3. The sun   4. Glasses
   5. Candles   6. A kite
   7. Carrots
E. 1. is a symbol of Canada
   2. has a beaver on its back
   3. build dams that become their homes
   4. are made of logs, sticks, and mud
   5. is important for swimming
F. (Answers will vary.)
G. (Answers will vary.)

11 Subject-Verb Agreement

A. 1. lays   2. has
   3. was   4. looks
   5. shines   6. burns
   7. rings   8. cuts
   9. rolls   10. glides
   11. flies
B. 1. hop   2. howl
   3. gallop   4. quack
   5. mew   6. bark
   7. waddle   8. climb
   9. slither   10. hoot
   11. swim   12. trumpet
   13. roar
C. 1. is   2. attracts
   3. sticks   4. has
   5. are ; have   6. are ; have
   7. attract
D. 1. flies   2. feeds
   3. fly   4. live
   5. are   6. eat ; catch
   7. is ; lays
E. 1. Chickens   2. duck
   3. ostrich   4. rooster
   5. owl

12 Adverbs and Modals

A. 1. happily   2. loudly
   3. neatly   4. slowly
   5. badly   6. proudly
   7. carefully   8. sadly
B. 1. carefully   2. timidly
   3. harshly   4. scarcely
   5. eagerly
C. (Answers will vary.)
D. 1. scarcely   2. carefully / timidly
   3. harshly   4. timidly / carefully
   5. eagerly
E. 1. May   2. can / may
   3. can   4. may
   5. May
F. (Answers will vary.)
G. 1. well   2. proudly
   3. hardly   4. boldly
   5. quietly   6. quickly
   7. loudly   8. clearly
   9. happily
H. 1. can   2. May
   3. Can   4. may
   5. can   6. Can
   7. May

13 Prepositions, Antonyms, Synonyms, and Homophones

A. 1. out   2. upon
   3. out   4. to
   5. with   6. of
   7. in   8. out
   9. with   10. out
B. 1. on top of   2. in front of
   3. beside   4. under
C. (Individual drawings)
D. (Suggested answers)
   1. old   2. slow
   3. noisy   4. out
   5. good   6. poor
E. (Suggested answers)
   1. small ; big   2. short ; on ; long
F. 1. under   2. big
   3. small   4. sad
   5. shut   6. loud
G. 1. blew   2. blue
   3. sea   4. see
   5. sun   6. son
H. 1. week   2. flower
   3. blew   4. see
   5. sun   6. deer

14 Question Starters, Proofreading, and Editing

A. (Suggested answers)
 2. When did they leave?
 3. Where was the hat?
 4. Who went to Alberta?
 5. When was Kathleen born?
 6. What did you make?

B. 1. Tomorrow is Easter Sunday.
 2. She goes to Vancouver every summer.
 3. Her birthday is February 3.
 4. Is Mr. Smith our new gym teacher?

C. 1. Who is your doctor?
 2. Don't do that!
 3. Take out the garbage.
 4. Where do you go on vacation?

D. The fourteenth of February is Valentine's Day. On Valentine's Day, lots of people give cards and gifts to one another. The heart is the symbol for this special day.

E. 1. flew   2. short
 3. leaf   4. wait
 5. raced   6. Flowers
 7. didn't

F. 1. North Pole   2. very
 3. called   4. there
 5. lot   6. ice
 7. for   8. other

G. Another name for the Antarctic is the South Pole. It is almost fully covered with ice and snow. Most of the ice has been on the ground for hundreds of years.

 Penguins live on and around the Antarctic. The Emperor and King Penguins live closest to the South Pole itself. Other penguins live near Australia and Argentina.

 The largest penguin is the Emperor and the smallest is the Blue Fairy.

Progress Test 2

A. 1. Don't   2. isn't
 3. weren't   4. hasn't
 5. couldn't   6. doesn't
 7. can't   8. won't
 9. shouldn't   10. Haven't
 11. Aren't   12. mustn't

B. 1. polar ; white   2. oily ; dry
 3. snowy ; far   4. long ; tall
 5. brown   6. several
 7. two   8. delicious
 9. Many   10. Some ; foul
 11. tough   12. many

C. 1. The holidays (were happy with lots of fun).
 2. People (were driving home for the week).

---

 3. Children (played in the snow).
 4. Shoppers (bundled their packages into cars).
 5. Stores (stayed open late).
 6. Houses (shone with lights).
 7. The season (is a time of joy).
 8. Trees (are decorated carefully).
 9. Cookies and cakes (are baked and ready to eat).
 10. People (think about others).
 11. They (wrap their gifts).
 12. Mothers, fathers, and children (spend time together).
 13. There (is peace for a little while everywhere).

D. 1. have   2. take
 3. carries   4. make
 5. attracts

E. 1. person   2. child
 3. mother   4. one
 5. girl

F. 1. may   2. quickly
 3. sadly   4. slowly
 5. can   6. proudly
 7. loudly   8. timidly
 9. badly   10. harshly
 11. hardly

G.

k	m	d	w	x	l	j	u	p	o	n	z	c	a	k
n	h	b	e	h	i	n	d	c	y	w	d	m	s	u
n	u	y	o	u	t	b	d	o	p	w	i	t	h	m
z	c	s	c	o	v	e	r	n	g	m	p	j	r	b
t	j	k	o	b	j	f	z	t	n	u	n	d	e	r
x	l	q	n	f	l	q	t	o	f	k	f	l	s	q
b	e	s	i	d	e	n	b	w	d	p	o	c	i	n

H. 1. A   2. A   3. H   4. A
 5. S   6. S   7. A   8. A
 9. A   10. A   11. A   12. H
 13. S   14. H   15. S   16. H

Section 3 — Answers

1 Creatures of the Galapagos Islands

A.

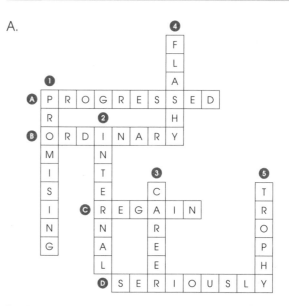

(Crossword grid)

Across:
- A. APPROXIMATELY
- B. EXPOSED
- C. BASKING
- D. HERBIVORE
- E. CREATURES

Down:
- 2. CHARACTERISTERISCC
- 4. AYY
- 3. EFFORTLESS
- 5. EXTRAORDINARY
- 1. UNIQUU
- SCALLY
- COLD-BLOODED
- LY

B. (Suggested answers)

Things that are different (Galapagos Tortoise) :
- short feet
- eats prickly pear cactus, fruits, ferns, leaves, and grasses
- over one metre long

Things that are the same :
- live on the Galapagos Islands
- enjoy basking in the sun
- reptile

Things that are different (Marine Iguana) :
- long claws
- eats marine algae and seaweed
- approximately one metre long

C. (Individual writing)

D. (Suggested answers)
1. monkey ; A monkey is not a reptile. ; alligator
2. Canada ; Canada is not an island. ; New Zealand
3. park ; A park is not a body of water. ; lake
4. shoe ; A shoe is not worn on the head. ; cap

2 Bet You Can't Eat Just One

A. 1. C
3. F
5. A
7. H
2. E
4. G
6. D
8. B

B. (Suggested answers)

George Crum ; Fussy diner

Potato chips were invented.

A restaurant in Saratoga Springs, New York

In 1853

In order to annoy a fussy diner, George Crum boiled potato slices which we know now as potato chips.

C. (Individual writing)

D. (Individual writing of each word in a sentence)
2. unimportant
3. unkind
4. untie
5. unfair
6. unpopular
7. unsafe
8. untrue

3 Barbie Hits the Track

A.

(Crossword grid)

Across:
- A. PROGRESSED
- B. ORDINARY
- C. REGAIN
- D. SERIOUSLY

Down:
- 4. FLAG
- 1. PROMISING
- 2. INTERNAL
- 3. CAREER
- 5. TROPHY

B. (Individual writing)

C. (Individual writing)

D. (Individual writing)

4 Wash Day

A. 1. shiny
2. allowed
3. First
4. Next
5. towel
6. rinsed
7. Lastly

8. bead

B. 1. next
   2. first
   3. last

C. (Individual writing)

D. 1. knew
   2. four
   3. weak
   4. pair
   5. hear

E. 1. The bee buzzed around the flower garden.
   2. The wind blew leaves onto the freshly washed car.
   3. Michael could see how special the car was to Larry.
   4. There were eight kittens at the pet store.
   5. Sandra walked to the store to buy milk.

F. 1. wall / talk
   2. fun
   3. nope / hose
   4. host / pose
   5. meat

Challenge
   (Individual writing)

5 Animal Pals

A. 1a. small   b. tiny
   2a. rely   b. need
   3a. eating   b. chewing
   4a. fur   b. coat
   5a. chum   b. pal

B. (Individual writing)

C.

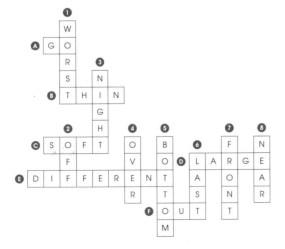

D. 1. B   2. D
   3. E   4. C

5. A   6. F

E. (Individual creation)

6 Penelope and Her Plastic Palm Tree

A. (Individual answers)
B. (Individual writing)
C. 1. palm
   2. parents
   3. Patterson
   4. Patty
   5. Paul
   6. Penelope
   7. pet
   8. Peterborough
   9. petition
   10. Pine
   11. placed
   12. plastic
   13. Poncho
   14. poodle
   15. Priscilla
   16. purple

D. 1. he's
   2. wouldn't
   3. they're
   4. I'll
   5. it's
   6. I'd

E. 1. could not
   2. we have
   3. I am
   4. she will
   5. that is
   6. you are

F. 1. I'll write a speech about my plastic palm tree.
   2. It wouldn't make sense to get rid of such a beautiful tree.

G. (Individual writing)

7 The Night the Lights Went out

A. 1. C   2. F
   3. H   4. B
   5. I   6. J

7. A   8. G

9. E   10. D

B. (Individual writing)

C. 1. downstairs

   2. paperback

   3. candlelight

   4. outside

   5. everyone

   6. himself

   7. newspaper

   8. fireplace

D. 1. friendly ; comfortable

   2. red ; dark

   3. tasty ; fresh

   4. wax ; orange

   5. playful ; rubber

   6. wonderful ; delicious

   7. noisy ; small

   8. tired ; cool

E. (Individual writing)

Progress Test 1

A. 1. tower

   2. guide

   3. traffic

   4. ancient

   5. fire

   6. candles

   7. invented

   8. brighter

   9. electricity

   10. original

B. 1. E   2. C

   3. F   4. H

   5. A   6. B

   7. D   8. G

C. 1. C   2. E

   3. F   4. B

   5. A   6. D

   7. H   8. G

D. (Suggested answers)

   1. elephant ; An elephant is not a pet. ; rabbit

   2. belt ; A belt is not worn on the feet. ; boot

   3. swimming ; Swimming does not involve a ball. ; football

E. 1. pear

   2. heard

   3. sail

   4. sun

   5. week

F. 1. sun

   2. nope / hose

   3. came

   4. rat / can

   5. pin

G. 1. C   2. E

   3. A   4. F

   5. D   6. B

H. 1. I'll

   2. You're

   3. that's

   4. they're

   5. I'm

   6. couldn't

I. 1. D   2. F

   3. A   4. G

   5. B   6. E

   7. H   8. C

J. (Individual writing of each word in a sentence)

   1. un<u>safe</u>

   2. un<u>lock</u>

   3. un<u>tie</u>

   4. un<u>tidy</u>

   5. un<u>happy</u>

K. 1. tall ; bright

   2. wise ; rocky

   3. playful ; blue

   4. tiny ; salty

   5. old ; wax

L. 1. famaly   → family

   2. wonderfull → wonderful

   3. whatching → watching

   4. reel   → real

   5. intresting → interesting

   6. freinds   → friends

8 The Three-Toed Sloth

A.

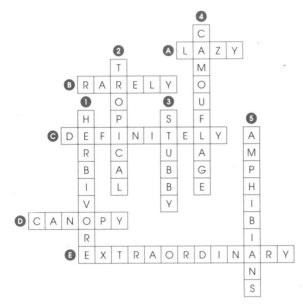

B. (Individual writing)

C. 1. A   2. F
  3. E   4. C
  5. B   6. D

D. (Individual drawings)

9 The Dead Sea

A. 1. C   2. F
  3. H   4. G
  5. A   6. B
  7. D   8. E

B. 2. 4   3. 2
  4. 3   5. 3
  6. 2   7. 2
  8. 3

Challenge

  evaporation / characteristics

C. 1. seas
  2. boxes
  3. bodies
  4. countries
  5. addresses
  6. lunches
  7. rivers
  8. wishes
  9. oceans
  10. buzzes

D. 1. lake
  2. guess
  3. berry
  4. peach
  5. lady
  6. fox
  7. tourist
  8. bush

E. (Individual answers)

10 The Story of Chocolate

A. 1. variety
  2. make
  3. outer
  4. rich
  5. valuable
  6. instant
  7. secret
  8. explorer
  9. delicious
  10. sip

B. (Individual answers)

C. (Individual answers)

Challenge

  (Suggested answers)

  cola ; hot ; hole ; coal ; lot ; cole ; cot ; eat ; ate ; tea ;
  hoe ; ale ; let ; tale ; hale ; hoot ; loot ; tool ; hoe

D. (Individual design)

11 Dr. Know-It-All

A. (Individual writing)

B. 1. dog
  2. an axe
  3. broom
  4. silk
  5. cat
  6. market
  7. tree
  8. freezer
  9. bicycle
  10. pie

C. (Suggested answers)

1. apple ; cherry ; peach
   They are all fruits.
2. water ; juice ; lemonade
   They are all things you can drink.
3. ice ; ice cream ; popsicle
   They are all things that are cold.
4. truck ; wagon ; bicycle
   They are all things with wheels.
5. book ; letter ; magazine
   They are all things that can be read.
D. 1. SHE HAD A PUMPKIN FOR A COACH
   2. MILK AND QUACKERS

12 Jim Carrey

A. 1. B 　　2. A
   3. B 　　4. A
   5. C 　　6. B
   7. A 　　8. B
B. (Individual writing)
C. 1. mechanic
   2. veterinarian
   3. reporter
   4. actor
   5. dentist
   6. comedian
   7. stylist
   8. pilot
D. (Individual writing)
E. (Individual drawing)

13 A Friendly Letter

A. (Individual writing)
B.

C. 1. its
   2. It's
   3. It's
   4. its
   5. its
   6. It's
Challenge
   (Individual writing)

14 A Tall Tale

A. 1. D 　　2. F
   3. E 　　4. B
   5. G 　　6. H
   7. A 　　8. C
B. (Individual writing)
C. 1. C 　　2. A
   3. D 　　4. E
   5. B
D. (Individual writing)
E. 1. She
   2. We
   3. It
   4. They
   5. You
F. 1. We are going out for dinner.
   2. He is my brother.
   3. It is very exciting to read.
   4. She is the best speller in the class.
   5. They went to watch the football game.

15 The Four-Star Ranch

A. 1. boots
   2. canteen
   3. hat
   4. horseshoe
   5. lope
   6. mane
   7. reins
   8. saddle
   9. trail
   10. trot
B. (Individual writing)
C. 1. They're

2. Their
3. there
4. there
5. Their
6. They're
7. their
8. there

D. 1. lamb
2. calf
3. kitten
4. chick
5. foal
6. kid

Progress Test 2

A. 1. tomato
2. bushels
3. pots
4. heat
5. picnic
6. sparkling
7. recipe
8. stirring
9. tasted
10. jars

B. 1. F   2. G
3. C   4. E
5. D   6. H
7. B   8. A

C. 1. boil
2. delicious
3. pasta
4. recipe
5. stove
6. tomato

D. 1. B   2. F
3. D   4. E
5. C   6. A

E. 1. 3   2. 4
3. 2   4. 5
5. 2   6. 3

F. (Suggested answers)
1. student ; teacher ; desk

They are things you find in a school.
2. pizza ; taco ; hamburger
They are things that you eat.
3. peas ; carrots ; spinach
They are all vegetables.

G. 1. match
2. spoon
3. market
4. van
5. bone

H. 1. tourists
2. lunches
3. countries
4. foxes
5. addresses
6. wishes
7. geese
8. women

I. 1. It's
2. its
3. They're
4. there
5. their

J. 1. She
2. They
3. He
4. We
5. It

K. 1. kitten
2. foal
3. kid
4. lamb

L. 1. A   2. D
3. B   4. C

M. 1. dentist
2. pilot
3. veterinarian
4. comedian

1.

2. 1. bark   2. trumpet
   3. quack   4. roar
   5. squeak   6. crow
   7. squeal   8. hoot
   9. mew

3.

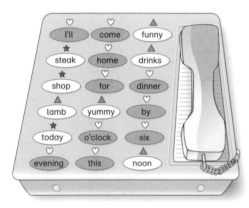

Message:
I'll come home for dinner by six o'clock this evening.

4.

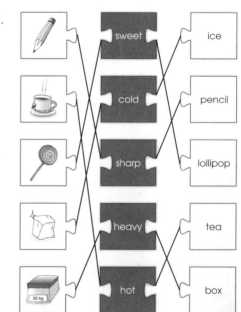

5.

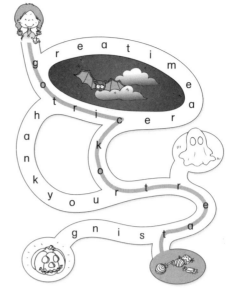

6.

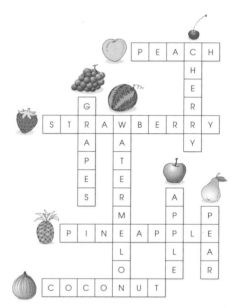

7.

(matching)
- sweet — lollipop
- cold — ice
- sharp — pencil
- heavy — box
- hot — tea

8. 1. I am eager to learn how to fly.
    2. I will fly when you say "magic".
    3. I know magic but I can't fly. /
       I can't fly but I know magic.

9.

g	o	l	c	v	b	s	k	u	n	k	i
n	c	h	e	e	t	a	h	g	m	h	d
l	f	a	y	r	j	v	c	l	k	c	x
i	k	g	i	r	a	f	f	e	p	h	e
o	a	h	k	a	p	e	n	g	u	i	n
n	n	d	b	c	a	u	c	i	t	m	c
b	g	e	m	c	h	x	o	w	a	p	a
d	a	j	g	o	k	t	e	b	q	a	r
c	r	o	c	o	d	i	l	e	s	n	i
j	o	z	f	n	t	g	m	a	f	z	b
e	o	a	o	d	z	e	b	r	a	e	o
k	b	e	a	v	e	r	h	i	b	e	u

10.

Christmas, glittering, mistletoe, festival, carol, tree, feast, decorate, present, Noel, gathering, holiday, tinsel, merry, family

11.

	¹W	E	A	S	E	L		²T		
	H					³F	I	N	D	
	I		⁴F		⁵F	U	N			
	⁶S	H	E	L	T	E	R			
	K		O		E		⁷F			
	E		P		⁸D	A	R	K		
	R		P				I			
	S		Y		⁹H	E	A	R		
							N			
							D			

12. (Individual drawings)

13.

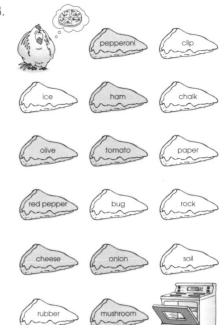

pepperoni, clip, ice, ham, chalk, olive, tomato, paper, red pepper, bug, rock, cheese, onion, soil, rubber, mushroom

14.

1. duckling
2. owlet
3. lamb
4. puppy
5. kitten
6. chick
7. cub
8. piglet
9. kid
10. calf

15.

o	p	e	t	a	m	h	g	n	t	a	c
e	g	t	r	a	p	e	z	o	i	d	k
c	o	l	e	n	p	x	a	c	t	a	g
c	i	r	c	l	e	a	n	t	r	t	b
r	p	e	t	a	s	g	u	a	e	r	o
s	q	u	a	r	e	o	a	g	o	i	r
t	u	i	n	g	e	n	g	o	y	a	j
a	e	t	g	n	o	x	d	n	t	n	e
r	a	z	l	i	a	g	n	i	a	g	u
e	h	p	e	n	t	a	g	o	n	l	m
c	t	d	i	m	u	p	e	d	l	e	q
h	n	a	l	s	f	e	d	p	i	v	t

16. 1. CUB 2. SUB
    3. SUN 4. BUN
    5. BUG 6. MUG

17.

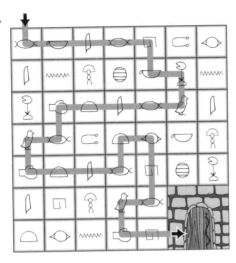

18. 1. honeycomb
    2. starfish
    3. keyboard
    4. headquarters
    5. firewood
    6. bookworm
    7. nutshell
    8. cupcake
    9. rainbow

19.

hark — lark — bark — shark — dark — spark — mark — back — park

20.

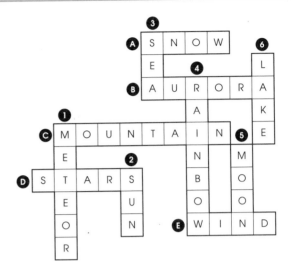

Across/Down crossword:
- A: S N O W
- B: A U R O R A
- C: M O U N T A I N
- D: S T A R S
- E: W I N D
- 3: S E A
- 6: L A K E
- 4: R A (...) — RAIN
- 1: M E T E O R
- 2: S U N
- 5: M O O N
- Column words: SNOWBALL, AURORA, MOUNTAIN, METEOR, STARS, SUN, MOON, WIND